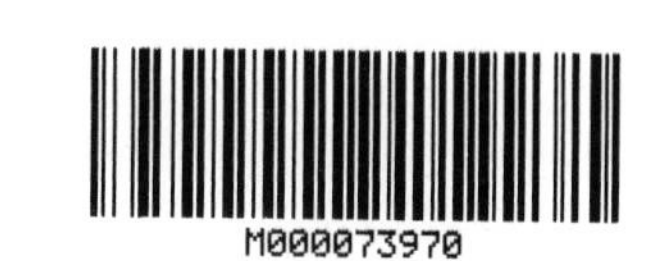

I ASK YOU TO PRAY FOR ME

I Ask You to Pray for Me

Opening a Horizon of Hope

POPE FRANCIS

Paulist Press
New York / Mahwah, NJ

Cover image courtesy of L'Osservatore Romano Photographic Service. All rights reserved.
Cover design by Sharyn Banks
Book design by Lynn Else

Library of Congress Cataloging-in-Publication Data

Francis, Pope, 1936–
[Vi chiedo di pregare per me. English]
I ask you to pray for me : opening a horizon of hope / Pope Francis.
pages cm
Includes bibliographical references.
ISBN 978-0-8091-4859-2 (alk. paper) — ISBN 978-1-58768-334-3
I. Title.
BX1378.7.A25 2013b
252`.02—dc23

2013025520

ISBN: 978-0-8091-4859-2 (paperback)
ISBN: 978-1-58768-334-3 (e-book)

Published by Paulist Press by special arrangement with Libreria Editrice Vaticana
997 Macarthur Boulevard
Mahwah, New Jersey 07430

www.paulistpress.com

Printed and bound in the
United States of America

Contents

Preface

Remain steadfast in the journey of faith, with firm hope in the Lord. This is the secret of our journey! He gives us the courage to swim against the tide...There are no difficulties, trials, or misunderstandings to fear, provided we remain united to God as branches to the vine, provided we do not lose our friendship with him, provided we make ever more room for him in our lives. This is especially so whenever we feel poor, weak, and sinful, because God grants strength to our weakness, riches to our poverty, conversion and forgiveness to our sinfulness. The Lord is so rich in mercy: if we go to him, he forgives us every time. Let us trust in God's work! With him, we can do great things; he will give us the joy of being his disciples, his witnesses. Commit yourselves to great ideals, to the most important things. We Christians were not chosen by the Lord for little things; push onward toward the highest principles. Stake your lives on noble ideals!

Let us open wide the door of our lives to the new things of God, which the Holy Spirit gives us. May he transform us, confirm us in our trials, strengthen our union with the Lord, our steadfastness in him: this is a true joy! So may it be.

I

Apostolic Blessing *Urbi et Orbi*

Brothers and Sisters, good evening!

You know that it was the duty of the Conclave to give Rome a Bishop. It seems that my brother Cardinals have gone to the ends of the earth to get one..., but here we are...I thank you for your welcome. The diocesan community of Rome now has its Bishop. Thank you! First of all, I would like to offer a prayer for our Bishop Emeritus, Benedict XVI. Let us pray together for him, that the Lord may bless him and that Our Lady may keep him.

Our Father, who art in heaven,
hallowed be thy name;
thy kingdom come;
thy will be done on earth as it is in heaven.
Give us this day our daily bread;
and forgive us our trespasses
as we forgive those who trespass
against us;
and lead us not into temptation,
but deliver us from evil.
Amen.

Hail Mary, full of grace, the Lord is with you;
blessed are you among women,
and blessed is the fruit of your womb, Jesus.
Holy Mary, Mother of God,
pray for us sinners
now and at the hour of our death.
Amen.

Glory be to the Father, the Son, and the Holy Spirit;
as it was in the beginning, is now, and ever shall be,
world without end.
Amen.

Now, we take up this journey: Bishop and People. This journey of the Church of Rome, which presides in charity over all the Churches. A journey of fraternity, of love, of trust among us. Let us always pray for one another. Let us pray for the whole world, that there may be a great spirit of fraternity. It is my hope for you that this journey of the Church, which we start today, and in which my Cardinal Vicar, here present, will assist me, will be fruitful for the evangelization of this most beautiful city.

II

Missa Pro Ecclesia with the Cardinal Electors

READINGS

FIRST READING

Isaiah 2:2–5

In days to come, the mountain of the LORD's house shall be established as the highest mountain and raised above the hills. All nations shall stream toward it. Many peoples shall come and say: "Come, let us go up to the LORD's mountain, to the house of the God of Jacob, that he may instruct us in his ways, and we may walk in his paths." For from Zion shall go forth instruction, and the word of the LORD from Jerusalem. He shall judge between the nations, and set terms for many peoples. They shall beat their swords into plowshares and their spears into pruning hooks; one nation shall not raise the sword against another, nor shall they train for war again. House of Jacob, come, let us walk in the light of the LORD!

PSALM

Psalm 97

The LORD is king; let the earth rejoice; let the many islands be glad. Cloud and darkness surround him; justice and right are the foundation of his throne. Fire goes before him, consuming his foes on every side. His lightening illumines the world; the earth sees and trembles. The mountains melt like wax before the LORD, before the Lord of all the earth. The heavens proclaim his justice; all peoples see his glory.

II

All who serve idols are put to shame, who glory in worthless things; all gods bow down before him. Zion hears and is glad, and the daughters of Judah rejoice because of your judgments, O LORD. For you, LORD, are the Most High over all the earth, exalted far above all gods. You who love the LORD, hate evil, he protects the souls of the faithful, rescues them from the hand of the wicked. Light dawns for the just, and gladness for the honest of heart. Rejoice in the LORD, you just, and give thanks at the remembrance of his holiness.

SECOND READING

1 Peter 2:4–9

Come to him, a living stone, rejected by human beings but chosen and precious in the sight of God, and, like living stones, let yourselves be built into a spiritual house to be a holy priesthood to offer spiritual sacrifices acceptable to God through Jesus Christ. For it says in scripture: "Behold, I am laying a stone in Zion, a cornerstone, chosen and precious, and whoever believes in it shall not be put to shame." Therefore, its value is for you who have faith, but for those without faith: "The stone which the builders rejected has become the cornerstone," and "A stone that will make people stumble, and a rock that will make them fall." They stumble by disobeying the word, as is their destiny. But you are "a chosen race, a royal priesthood, a holy nation, a people of his own, so that you may announce the praises" of him who called you out of darkness into his wonderful light.

GOSPEL

Matthew 16:13–19

When Jesus went into the region of Caesarea Philippi he asked his disciples, "Who do people say that the Son of Man is?" They replied, "Some say John the Baptist, others Elijah, still others Jeremiah or one of the prophets." He said to them, "But who do you say that I am?" Simon Peter said in reply, "You are the Messiah, the Son of the living God." Jesus said to him in reply, "Blessed are you, Simon son of Jonah. For flesh and blood has not revealed this to you, but my heavenly Father. And so I say to you, you are Peter, and upon this rock I will build my church, and the gates of the netherworld shall not prevail against it. I will give you the keys to the kingdom of heaven. Whatever you bind on earth shall be bound in heaven; and whatever you loose on earth shall be loosed in heaven."

HOMILY

In these three readings, I see a common element: that of movement. In the first reading, it is the movement of a journey; in the second reading, the movement of building the Church; in the third, in the Gospel, the movement involved in professing the faith. Journeying, building, professing.

Journeying. "O house of Jacob, come, let us walk in the light of the Lord" (Isa 2:5). This is the first thing that God said to Abraham: Walk in my presence and live blamelessly. Journeying: our life is a journey, and when we stop moving, things go wrong. Always journeying, in the presence of the Lord, in the light of the Lord, seeking to live with the blamelessness that God asked of Abraham in his promise.

Building. Building the Church. We speak of stones: stones are solid; but living stones, stones anointed by the

Holy Spirit. Building the Church, the Bride of Christ, on the cornerstone that is the Lord himself. This is another kind of movement in our lives: building.

Thirdly, professing. We can walk as much as we want, we can build many things, but if we do not profess Jesus Christ, things go wrong. We may become a charitable NGO, but not the Church, the Bride of the Lord. When we are not walking, we stop moving. When we are not building on the stones, what happens? The same thing that happens to children on the beach when they build sandcastles: everything is swept away, there is no solidity. When we do not profess Jesus Christ, the saying of Léon Bloy comes to mind: "Anyone who does not pray to the Lord prays to the devil." When we do not profess Jesus Christ, we profess the worldliness of the devil, a demonic worldliness.

Journeying, building, professing. But things are not so straightforward, because in journeying, building, professing, there can sometimes be jolts, movements that are not properly part of the journey: movements that pull us back.

This Gospel continues with a situation of a particular kind. The same Peter who professed Jesus Christ, now says to him: You are the Christ, the Son of the living God. I will follow you, but let us not speak of the Cross. That has nothing to do with it. I will follow you on other terms, but without the Cross. When we journey without the Cross, when we build without the Cross, when we profess Christ without the Cross, we are not disciples of the Lord, we are worldly: we may be bishops, priests, cardinals, popes, but not disciples of the Lord.

My wish is that all of us, after these days of grace, will have the courage, yes, the courage, to walk in the presence of the Lord, with the Lord's Cross; to build the Church on the Lord's blood, which was poured out on the Cross; and to profess the one glory: Christ crucified. And in this way, the Church will go forward.

My prayer for all of us is that the Holy Spirit, through the intercession of the Blessed Virgin Mary, our Mother, will grant us this grace: to walk, to build, to profess Jesus Christ crucified. Amen.

III

Audience with the College of Cardinals

Dear Brother Cardinals,

The period of the conclave has been a momentous time, not only for the College of Cardinals, but also for all the faithful. In these days, we have felt almost tangibly the affection and the solidarity of the universal Church, as well as the concern of so many people who, even if they do not share our faith, look to the Church and the Holy See with respect and admiration. From every corner of the earth, fervent prayers have been offered up by the Christian people for the new Pope, and my first encounter with the thronging crowd in Saint Peter's Square was deeply moving. With that evocative image of the people gathered in joyful prayer still impressed on my memory, I want to express my sincere thanks to the bishops, priests, consecrated persons, young people, families, and the elderly for their spiritual closeness, so touching and so deeply felt.

I want to express my sincere and profound gratitude to all of you, my dear venerable brother Cardinals, for your ready cooperation in the task of leading the Church during the period of the *Sede Vacante*. I greet each one of you warmly, beginning with the Dean of the College of Cardinals, Cardinal Angelo Sodano, whom I thank for his devoted words and his fervent good wishes addressed to me on behalf of all of you. I also thank Cardinal Tarcisio Bertone, Camerlengo of the Holy Roman Church, for his attentive service during this transitional period, as well as our dear friend Cardinal Giovanni Battista Re, who led us during the conclave: thank you very much! My thoughts turn with particular affection to the Cardinals who, on account of age or ill health, made their contribution and expressed their love for the Church by offering up their sufferings and their prayers. And I should tell you that the day before yesterday, Cardinal Mejia had a heart attack and was taken to the Pio XI Hospital. But they think his condition is stable, and he has sent us his greetings.

Nor can I omit to thank all those who carried out various tasks in the preparation and the conduct of the conclave, providing the Cardinals with security and peace of mind in this period of such importance for the life of the Church.

My thoughts turn with great affection and profound gratitude to my venerable Predecessor, Benedict XVI, who enriched and invigorated the Church during the years of his Pontificate by his teaching, his goodness, his leadership, his faith, his humility, and his meekness. All this remains as a spiritual patrimony for us all. The Petrine ministry, lived with total dedication, found in him a wise and humble exponent, his gaze always firmly on Christ, the risen Christ, present and alive in the Eucharist. We will always accompany him with fervent prayers, with constant remembrance, with undying and affectionate gratitude. We feel that Benedict XVI has kindled a flame deep within our hearts: a flame that will continue to burn because it will be fed by his prayers, which continue to sustain the Church on her spiritual and missionary path.

Dear brother Cardinals, this meeting of ours is intended to be, as it were, a prolongation of the intense ecclesial communion we have experienced during this period. Inspired by a profound sense of responsibility and supported by a great love for Christ and for the Church, we have prayed together, fraternally sharing our feelings, our experiences and reflections. In this atmosphere of great warmth, we have come to know one another better in a climate of mutual openness; and this is good, because we are brothers. Someone said to me: the Cardinals are the priests of the Holy Father. That community, that friendship, that closeness will do us all good. And our acquaintance and mutual openness have helped us to be docile to the action of the Holy Spirit. He, the Paraclete, is the ultimate source of every initiative and manifestation of faith. It is a curious thing: it makes me think of this. The Paraclete creates all the differences among the Churches, almost as if he were an Apostle of Babel. But on the other hand, it is he who creates unity from these differences, not in "equality," but in harmony. I remember the Father of the Church who described him thus: "*Ipse harmonia est.*" The Paraclete, who gives different charisms to each of us, unites us in this community of the Church, which worships the Father, the Son, and Him, the Holy Spirit.

On the basis of the authentic affective collegiality that unites the College of Cardinals, I express my desire to serve the Gospel with renewed love, helping the Church to become increasingly, in Christ and with Christ, the fruitful vine of the Lord. Inspired also by the celebration of the Year of Faith, all of us together, pastors and members of the faithful, will strive to respond faithfully to the Church's perennial mission: to bring Jesus Christ to mankind and to lead mankind to an encounter with Jesus Christ, the Way, the Truth, and the Life, truly present in the Church and also in every person. This meeting leads us to become new men in the mystery of Grace, kindling in the spirit that Christian joy that is the hundredfold given by Christ to those who welcome him into their lives.

As Pope Benedict XVI reminded us so many times in his teachings, and at the end, by his courageous and humble gesture, it is Christ who leads the Church through his Spirit. The Holy Spirit is the soul of the Church through his life-giving and unifying force: out of many, he makes one single body, the Mystical Body of Christ. Let us never yield to pessimism, to that bitterness that the devil offers us every day; let us not yield to pessimism or discouragement: let us be quite certain that the Holy Spirit bestows upon the Church, with his powerful breath, the courage to persevere and also to seek new methods of evangelization, so as to bring the Gospel to the uttermost ends of the earth (cf. Acts 1:8). Christian truth is attractive and persuasive because it responds to the profound need of human life, proclaiming convincingly that Christ is the one Savior of the whole man and of all men. This proclamation remains as valid today as it was at the origin of Christianity, when the first great missionary expansion of the Gospel took place.

Dear brother Cardinals, take courage! Half of us are advanced in age. Old age is—as I like to say—the seat of life's wisdom. The old have acquired the wisdom that comes from having journeyed through life, like the old man Simeon, the old prophetess Anna in the Temple. And that wisdom enabled them to recognize Jesus. Let us pass on this wisdom to the young: like good wine that improves with age, let us give life's wisdom to the young. I am reminded of a German poet who said of old age: *Es ist ruhig, das Alter, und fromm*: it is a time of tranquility and prayer. And also a time to pass on this wisdom to the young. You will now return to your respective sees to continue your ministry, enriched by the experience of these days, so full of faith and ecclesial communion. This unique and incomparable experience has enabled us to grasp deeply all the beauty of the Church, which is a glimpse of the radiance of the risen Christ: one day we will gaze upon that beautiful face of the risen Christ!

I entrust my ministry and your ministry to the powerful intercession of Mary, our Mother, Mother of the Church. Under her maternal gaze, may each one of you continue gladly along your path, attentive to the voice of her divine Son, strengthening your unity, persevering in your common prayer, and bearing witness to the true faith in the constant presence of the Lord. With these sentiments, which I really mean, I impart a heartfelt Apostolic Blessing, which I extend to your co-workers and to all those entrusted to your pastoral care.

IV

Audience with Representatives of the Communications Media

Dear Friends,

At the beginning of my ministry in the See of Peter, I am pleased to meet all of you who have worked here in Rome throughout this intense period, which began with the unexpected announcement made by my venerable Predecessor, Benedict XVI, on 11 February last. To each of you, I offer a cordial greeting.

The role of the mass media has expanded immensely in these years, so much so that they are an essential means of informing the world about the events of contemporary history. I would like, then, to thank you in a special way for the professional coverage, which you provided during these days—you really worked, didn't you?—when the eyes of the whole world, and not just those of Catholics, were turned to the Eternal City and particularly to this place, which has, as its heart, the tomb of Saint Peter. Over the past few weeks, you have had to provide information about the Holy See and about the Church, her rituals and traditions, her faith, and above all, the role of the Pope and his ministry.

I am particularly grateful to those who viewed and presented these events of the Church's history in a way which was sensitive to the right context in which they need to be read, namely that of faith. Historical events almost always demand a nuanced interpretation, which, at times, can also take into account the dimension of faith. Ecclesial events are certainly no more intricate than political or economic events! But they do have one particular underlying feature: they follow a pattern which does not readily correspond to the "worldly" categories which we are accustomed to use, and so it is not easy to interpret and communicate them to a wider and more varied public. The Church is certainly a human and historical institution with all that that entails, yet, her nature is not essentially political but spiritual: the Church is the People of God, the Holy People of God making its way to encounter Jesus Christ. Only from this perspective, can a satisfactory account be given of the Church's life and activity.

Christ is the Church's Pastor, but his presence in history passes through the freedom of human beings; from their midst one is chosen to serve as his Vicar, the Successor of the Apostle Peter. Yet, Christ remains the center, not the Successor of Peter: Christ, Christ is the center. Christ is the fundamental point of reference, the heart of the Church. Without him, Peter and the Church would not exist or have reason to exist. As Benedict XVI frequently reminded us, Christ is present in Church and guides her. In everything that has occurred, the principal agent has been, in the final analysis, the Holy Spirit. He prompted the decision of Benedict XVI for the good of the Church; he guided the Cardinals in prayer and in the election.

It is important, dear friends, to take into due account this way of looking at things, this hermeneutic, in order to bring into proper focus what really happened in these days.

All of this leads me to thank you once more for your work in these particularly demanding days, but also to ask you to try to understand more fully the true nature of the Church, as well as her journey in this world, with her virtues and her sins, and to know the spiritual concerns which guide her and are the most genuine way to understand her. Be assured that the Church, for her part, highly esteems your important work. At your disposal, you have the means to hear and to give voice to people's expectations and demands, and to provide for an analysis and interpretation of current events. Your work calls for careful preparation, sensitivity, and experience, like so many other professions, but it also demands a particular concern for what is true, good, and beautiful. This is something which we have in common, since the Church exists to communicate precisely this: Truth, Goodness, and Beauty "in person." It should be apparent that all of us are called, not to communicate ourselves, but this existential triad made up of truth, beauty, and goodness.

Some people wanted to know why the Bishop of Rome wished to be called Francis. Some thought of Francis Xavier, Francis De Sales, and also Francis of Assisi. I will tell you the story. During the election, I was seated next to the Archbishop Emeritus of São Paolo and Prefect Emeritus of the Congregation for the Clergy, Cardinal Claudio Hummes: a good friend, a good friend! When things were looking dangerous, he encouraged me. And when the votes reached two thirds, there was the usual applause, because the Pope had been elected. And he gave me a hug and a kiss, and said: "Don't forget the poor!" And those words came to me: the poor, the poor. Then, right away, thinking of the poor, I thought of Francis of Assisi. Then I thought of all the wars, as the votes were still being counted, till the end. Francis is also the man of peace. That is how the name came into my heart: Francis of Assisi. For me, he is the man of poverty, the man of peace, the man who loves and protects creation;

these days we do not have a very good relationship with creation, do we? He is the man who gives us this spirit of peace, the poor man...How I would like a Church which is poor and for the poor! Afterward, people were joking with me. "But you should call yourself Hadrian, because Hadrian VI was the reformer, we need a reform...." And someone else said to me: "No, no: your name should be Clement." "But why?" "Clement XV: thus you pay back Clement XIV who suppressed the Society of Jesus!" These were jokes. I love all of you very much, I thank you for everything you have done. I pray that your work will always be serene and fruitful, and that you will come to know ever better the Gospel of Jesus Christ and the rich reality of the Church's life. I commend you to the intercession of the Blessed Virgin Mary, Star of Evangelization, and with cordial good wishes for you and your families, each of your families. I cordially impart to all of you my blessing. Thank you.

(In Spanish)

Les dije que les daba de corazón la bendición. Como muchos de ustedes no pertenecen a la Iglesia católica, otros no son creyentes, de corazón doy esta bendición en silencio a cada uno de ustedes, respetando la conciencia de cada uno, pero sabiendo que cada uno de ustedes es hijo de Dios. Que Dios los bendiga!

[I told you I was cordially imparting my blessing. Since many of you are not members of the Catholic Church, and others are not believers, I cordially give this blessing silently, to each of you, respecting the conscience of each, but in the knowledge that each of you is a child of God. May God bless you!]

V

Holy Mass in the Parish of St. Anna

READINGS

FIRST READING

Isaiah 43:16–21

Thus says the LORD, who opens a way in the sea and a path in the mighty waters, who leads out chariots and horsemen, a powerful army, till they lie prostrate together, never to rise, snuffed out and quenched like a wick.

Remember not the events of the past, the things of long ago consider not; see, I am doing something new! Now it springs forth, do you not perceive it? In the desert I make a way, in the wasteland, rivers. Wild beasts honor me, jackals and ostriches, for I put water in the desert and rivers in the wasteland for my chosen people to drink, the people whom I formed for myself, that they might announce my praise.

PSALM

Psalm 126:1–2, 2–3, 4–5, 6

When the LORD brought back the captives of Zion, we were like men dreaming. Then our mouth was filled with laughter, and our tongue with rejoicing. Then they said among the nations, "The LORD has done great things for them."

The LORD has done great things for us; we are glad indeed. Restore our fortunes, O LORD, like the torrents in the southern desert. Those that sow in tears shall reap rejoicing. Although they go forth weeping, carrying the seed to be sown, They shall come back rejoicing, carrying their sheaves.

SECOND READING

Philippians 3:8–14

Brothers and sisters:

I consider everything as a loss because of the supreme good of knowing Christ Jesus my Lord. For his sake I have accepted the loss of all things and I consider them so much rubbish, that I may gain Christ and be found in him, not having any righteousness of my own based on the law but that which comes through faith in Christ, the righteousness from God, depending on faith to know him and the power of his resurrection and the sharing of his sufferings by being conformed to his death, if somehow I may attain the resurrection from the dead.

It is not that I have already taken hold of it or have already attained perfect maturity, but I continue my pursuit in hope that I may possess it, since I have indeed been taken possession of by Christ Jesus.

Brothers and sisters, I for my part do not consider myself to have taken possession.

Just one thing: forgetting what lies behind but straining forward to what lies ahead,

I continue my pursuit toward the goal, the prize of God's upward calling, in Christ Jesus.

GOSPEL

John 8:1–11

Jesus went to the Mount of Olives. But early in the morning he arrived again in the temple area, and all the people started coming to him, and he sat down and taught them. Then the scribes and the Pharisees brought a woman who had been caught in adultery and made her stand in the middle.

They said to him, "Teacher, this woman was caught in the very act of committing adultery. Now in the law, Moses commanded us to stone such women. So what do you say?" They said this to test him, so that they could have some charge to bring against him.

Jesus bent down and began to write on the ground with his finger. But when they continued asking him, he straightened up and said to them, "Let the one among you who is without sin be the first to throw a stone at her."

Again he bent down and wrote on the ground. And in response, they went away one by one, beginning with the elders. So he was left alone with the woman before him.

Then Jesus straightened up and said to her, "Woman, where are they? Has no one condemned you?" She replied, "No one, sir." Then Jesus said, "Neither do I condemn you. Go, and from now on do not sin anymore."

HOMILY

This is a beautiful story. First, we have Jesus alone on the mountain, praying. He was praying alone (cf. John 8:1). Then he went back to the Temple, and all the people went to him (cf. v. 2). Jesus in the midst of the people. And then, at the end, they left him alone with the woman (cf. v. 9). That solitude of Jesus! But it is a fruitful solitude: the solitude of prayer with the Father, and the beautiful solitude that is the Church's message for today: the solitude of his mercy toward this woman.

And among the people, we see a variety of attitudes: there were all the people who went to him; he sat and began to teach them: the people who wanted to hear the words of Jesus, the people with open hearts, hungry for the word of God. There were others who did not hear anything, who could not hear anything; and there were those who brought along this woman: Listen, Master, this woman has done such and such... we must do what Moses commanded us to do with women like this (cf. vv. 4–5).

I think we, too, are the people who, on the one hand want to listen to Jesus, but on the other hand, at times, like to find a stick to beat others with, to condemn others. And Jesus has this message for us: mercy. I think—and I say it with humility—that this is the Lord's most powerful message: mercy. It was he himself who said: "I did not come for the righteous." The righteous justify themselves. Go on, then, even if you can do it, I cannot! But they believe they can. "I came for sinners" (Mark 2:17).

Think of the gossip after the call of Matthew: he associates with sinners! (cf. Mark 2:16). He comes for us, when we recognize that we are sinners. But if we are like the Pharisee, before the altar, who said: I thank you Lord, that I am not like other men, and especially not like the one at the door, like that publican (cf. Luke 18:11–12), then we do not know the Lord's heart, and we will never have the joy of experiencing this mercy! It is not easy to entrust oneself to God's mercy, because it is an abyss beyond our comprehension. But we must! "Oh, Father, if you knew my life, you would not say that to me!" "Why, what have you done?" "Oh, I am a great sinner!" "All the better! Go to Jesus: he likes you to tell him these things!" He forgets, he has a very special capacity for forgetting. He forgets, he kisses you, he embraces you, and he simply says to you: "Neither do I condemn you; go, and sin no more" (John 8:11). That is the only advice he gives you. After a month, if we are in the same situation...Let us go back to the Lord. The Lord never tires of forgiving: never! It is we who tire of asking his forgiveness. Let us ask for the grace not to tire of asking forgiveness, because he never tires of forgiving. Let us ask for this grace.

*

WORDS AT THE END OF THE HOLY MASS

At the end of Mass, the parish priest of St. Anne in the Vatican, Father Bruno Silverstrini, OSA, and the Vicar General of His Holiness for Vatican City, Cardinal Angelo Comastri, directed their greetings to Pope Francis. The Holy Father concluded with these words:

There are some here who are not parishioners, including a few from Argentina—one is my Auxiliary Bishop—but today they are parishioners. I want to introduce to you a priest who comes from far away, a priest who works with children and with drug addicts on the street. He opened a school for them; he has done many things to make Jesus known, and all those boys and girls off the street, they today work with the studies they have done; they have the ability to work, they believe, and they love Jesus. I ask you Gonzalo, come greet the people: pray for him. He works in Uruguay; he is the founder of Jubilar Juan Pablo II. This is his work. I do not know how he came here, but I will find out! Thank you. Pray for him.

VI
Angelus

Brothers and Sisters, good morning!

After our first meeting last Wednesday, today, I can once again address my greeting to you all! And I am glad to do so on a Sunday, on the Lord's Day! This is beautiful and important for us Christians: to meet on Sundays, to greet each other, to speak to each other as we are doing now, in the square. A square which, thanks to the media, has global dimensions.

On this Fifth Sunday of Lent, the Gospel presents to us the episode of the adulterous woman (cf. John 8:1–11), whom Jesus saves from being condemned to death. Jesus' attitude is striking: we do not hear words of scorn, we do not hear words of condemnation, but only words of love, of mercy, which are an invitation to conversion. "Neither do I condemn you; go, and do not sin again" (v. 11). Ah! Brothers and sisters, God's face is the face of a merciful father who is always patient. Have you thought about God's patience, the patience he has with each one of us? That is his mercy. He always has patience, patience with us, he understands us, he waits for us, he does not tire of forgiving us if we are able to return to him with a contrite heart. "Great is God's mercy," says the Psalm.

In the past few days, I have been reading a book by a Cardinal—Cardinal Kasper, a clever theologian, a good theologian—on mercy. And that book did me a lot of good, but do not think I am promoting my cardinals' books! Not at all! Yet, it has done me so much good, so much good . . . Cardinal Kasper said that feeling mercy, that this word changes everything. This is the best thing we can feel: it changes the world. A little mercy makes the world less cold and more just. We need to understand properly this mercy of God, this merciful Father who is so patient. . . . Let us remember the Prophet Isaiah who says that even if our sins were scarlet, God's love would make them white as snow. This mercy is beautiful! I remember when I had only just become a bishop in the year 1992, the statue of Our Lady of Fatima had just arrived in Buenos Aires and a big Mass was celebrated for the sick. I went to hear confessions at that Mass. And almost at the end of the Mass, I stood up, because I had to go and administer a First Confirmation. And an elderly woman approached me, humble, very humble, and over eighty years old. I looked at her, and I said, "Grandmother"—because in our country that is how we address the elderly—do you want to make your confession?". "Yes," she said to me. "But if you have not sinned. . . ." And she said to me: "We all have sins. . . ." "But perhaps the Lord does not forgive them." "The Lord forgives all things," she said to me with conviction. "But how do you know, Madam?" "If the Lord did not forgive everything, the world would not exist." I felt an urge to ask her: "Tell me, Madam, did you study at the Gregorian [University]?", because that is the wisdom which the Holy Spirit gives: inner wisdom focused on God's mercy. Let us not forget this word: God never ever tires of forgiving us! "Well, Father, what is the problem?" Well, the problem is that we ourselves tire, we do not want to ask, we grow weary of asking for forgiveness. He never tires of forgiving, but at times we get tired of asking for forgiveness.

Let us never tire, let us never tire! He is the loving Father who always pardons, who has that heart of mercy for us all. And let us too learn to be merciful to everyone. Let us invoke the intercession of Our Lady who held in her arms the Mercy of God made man.

Let us now all pray the Angelus together:

V. The Angel of the Lord declared unto Mary.
R. And she conceived of the Holy Spirit.

Hail, Mary, full of grace, the Lord is with thee.
Blessed art thou among women,
and blessed is the fruit of thy womb, Jesus.
Holy Mary, Mother of God,
pray for us sinners,
now and at the hour of our death. Amen.

V. Behold the handmaid of the Lord.
R. Be it done unto me according to thy word.

Hail Mary.

V. And the Word was made flesh.
R. And dwelt among us.

Hail Mary.

V. Pray for us, O holy Mother of God.
R. That we may be made worthy of the promises of Christ.

Let us pray;
Pour forth, we beseech thee, O Lord, thy grace into our hearts; that we, to whom the Incarnation of Christ, thy Son, was made known by the message of an angel, may by his Passion and Cross be

brought to the glory of his Resurrection. Through the same Christ, our Lord.
Amen.

Glory be to the Father
and to the Son
and to the Holy Spirit,
as it was in the beginning
is now, and ever shall be
world without end. Amen.

AFTER THE ANGELUS:

I address a cordial greeting to all the pilgrims. Thank you for your welcome and for your prayers. Pray for me, I ask it of you. I renew my embrace of the faithful of Rome and I extend it to all of you, who come from various parts of Italy and of the world, as well as to all those who have joined us through the media.

I have chosen the name of the Patron of Italy, St. Francis of Assisi, and this strengthens my spiritual ties with this country where, as you know, my family comes from. However, Jesus has called us to belong to a new family: his Church, to this family of God, walking together on the path of the Gospel. May the Lord bless you and may Our Lady keep you. Do not forget this: the Lord never tires of forgiving! It is we who tire of asking forgiveness.

Have a good Sunday and a good lunch!

VII

Mass, Imposition of the Pallium and Bestowal of the Fisherman's Ring for the Beginning of the Petrine Ministry of the Bishop of Rome

READINGS

FIRST READING

2 Samuel 7:4–5, 12–14, 16

The word of the LORD came to Nathan:

"Go and tell my servant David, 'Thus the LORD speaks: When your days are ended and you are laid to rest with your ancestors, I will preserve the offspring of your body after you and make his sovereignty secure. It is he who shall build a house for my name, and I will make his royal throne secure forever. I will be a father to him and he a son to me. Your House and your sovereignty will always stand secure before me and your throne be established forever.'"

PSALM

Psalm 88

I will sing forever of your love, O LORD; through all ages my mouth will proclaim your truth. Of this I am sure, that your love lasts forever, that your truth is firmly established as the heavens.

I have made a covenant with my chosen one; I have sworn to David my servant: I will establish your dynasty forever and set up your throne through all ages.

He will say to me: 'You are my father, my God, the rock who saves me.' I will keep my love for him always; with him my covenant shall last.

SECOND READING

Romans 4:13, 16–18, 22

The promise of inheriting the world was not made to Abraham and his descendants on account of any law but on account of the righteousness which consists in faith. That is why what fulfills the promise depends on faith, so that it may be a free gift and be available to all of Abraham's descendants, not only those who belong to the Law but also those who belong to the faith of Abraham who is the father of all of us. As scripture says: I have made you the ancestor of many nations—Abraham is our father in the eyes of God, in whom he put his faith, and who brings the dead to life and calls into being what does not exist. Though it seemed Abraham's hope could not be fulfilled, he hoped and he believed, and through doing so he did become the father of many nations exactly as he had been promised: Your descendants will be as many as the stars. This is the faith that was "considered as justifying him."

GOSPEL

Matthew 1:16, 18–21, 24a

Jacob was the father of Joseph the husband of Mary; of her was born Jesus who is called Christ.

This is how Jesus Christ came to be born. His mother Mary was betrothed to Joseph; but before they came to live together she was found to be with child through the Holy Spirit. Her husband Joseph; being a man of honor and wanting to spare her publicity, decided to divorce her informally. He had made up his mind to do this when the angel of the Lord appeared to him in a dream and said, "Joseph son of David, do not be afraid to take Mary home as your wife, because she has conceived what is in her by the Holy Spirit. She will give birth to a son and you must name him Jesus, because he is the one who is to save his people from their sins." When Joseph woke up he did what the angel of the Lord had told him to do.

HOMILY

Dear Brothers and Sisters,

I thank the Lord that I can celebrate this Holy Mass for the inauguration of my Petrine ministry on the solemnity of Saint Joseph, the spouse of the Virgin Mary and the patron of the universal Church. It is a significant coincidence, and it is also the name-day of my venerable predecessor: we are close to him with our prayers, full of affection and gratitude.

I offer a warm greeting to my brother cardinals and bishops, the priests, deacons, men and women religious, and all the lay faithful. I thank the representatives of the other Churches and ecclesial Communities, as well as the representatives of the Jewish community and the other religious communities, for their presence. My cordial greetings go to the Heads of State and Government, the members of the official Delegations from many countries throughout the world, and the Diplomatic Corps.

In the Gospel, we heard that "Joseph did as the angel of the Lord commanded him and took Mary as his wife" (Matt 1:24). These words already point to the mission which

God entrusts to Joseph: he is to be the *custos*, the protector. The protector of whom? Of Mary and Jesus; but this protection is then extended to the Church, as Blessed John Paul II pointed out: "Just as Saint Joseph took loving care of Mary and gladly dedicated himself to Jesus Christ's upbringing, he likewise watches over and protects Christ's Mystical Body, the Church, of which the Virgin Mary is the exemplar and model" (*Redemptoris Custos*, 1).

How does Joseph exercise his role as protector? Discreetly, humbly, and silently, but with an unfailing presence and utter fidelity, even when he finds it hard to understand. From the time of his betrothal to Mary until the finding of the twelve-year-old Jesus in the Temple of Jerusalem, he is there at every moment with loving care. As the spouse of Mary, he is at her side in good times and bad, on the journey to Bethlehem for the census and in the anxious and joyful hours when she gave birth; amid the drama of the flight into Egypt and during the frantic search for their child in the Temple; and later in the day-to-day life of the home of Nazareth, in the workshop where he taught his trade to Jesus.

How does Joseph respond to his calling to be the protector of Mary, Jesus, and the Church? By being constantly attentive to God, open to the signs of God's presence and receptive to God's plans, and not simply to his own. This is what God asked of David, as we heard in the first reading. God does not want a house built by men, but faithfulness to his word, to his plan. It is God himself who builds the house, but from living stones sealed by his Spirit. Joseph is a "protector" because he is able to hear God's voice and be guided by his will; and for this reason, he is all the more sensitive to the persons entrusted to his safekeeping. He can look at things realistically, he is in touch with his surroundings, he can make truly wise decisions. In him, dear friends, we learn how to respond to God's call, readily and willingly, but we also see the core of the Christian vocation, which is Christ! Let us protect Christ in our lives, so that we can protect others, so that we can protect creation!

The vocation of being a "protector," however, is not just something involving us Christians alone; it also has a prior dimension which is simply human, involving everyone. It means protecting all creation, the beauty of the created world, as the Book of Genesis tells us and as Saint Francis of Assisi showed us. It means respecting each of God's creatures and respecting the environment in which we live. It means protecting people, showing loving concern for each and every person, especially children, the elderly, those in need, who are often the last we think about. It means caring for one another in our families: husbands and wives first protect one another, and then, as parents, they care for their children, and children themselves, in time, protect their parents. It means building sincere friendships in which we protect one another in trust, respect, and goodness. In the end, everything has been entrusted to our protection, and all of us are responsible for it. Be protectors of God's gifts!

Whenever human beings fail to live up to this responsibility, whenever we fail to care for creation and for our brothers and sisters, the way is opened to destruction and hearts are hardened. Tragically, in every period of history, there are "Herods" who plot death, wreak havoc, and mar the countenance of men and women.

Please, I would like to ask all those who have positions of responsibility in economic, political, and social life, and all men and women of goodwill: let us be "protectors" of creation, protectors of God's plan inscribed in nature, protectors of one another and of the environment. Let us not allow omens of destruction and death to accompany the advance of this world! But to be "protectors," we also have to keep watch over ourselves! Let us not forget that hatred, envy, and pride defile our lives! Being protectors, then, also means keeping watch over our emotions, over our hearts, because they are the seat of good and evil intentions: intentions that build up and tear down! We must not be afraid of goodness or even tenderness!

Here, I would add one more thing: caring, protecting demands goodness, it calls for a certain tenderness. In the Gospels, Saint Joseph appears as a strong and courageous man, a working man, yet, in his heart, we see great tenderness, which is not the virtue of the weak but rather a sign of strength of spirit and a capacity for concern, for compassion, for genuine openness to others, for love. We must not be afraid of goodness, of tenderness!

Today, together with the feast of Saint Joseph, we are celebrating the beginning of the ministry of the new Bishop of Rome, the Successor of Peter, which also involves a certain power. Certainly, Jesus Christ conferred power upon Peter, but what sort of power was it? Jesus' three questions to Peter about love are followed by three commands: feed my lambs, feed my sheep. Let us never forget that authentic power is service, and that the Pope, too, when exercising power, must enter ever more fully into that service, which has its radiant culmination on the Cross. He must be inspired by the lowly, concrete, and faithful service which marked Saint Joseph and, like him, he must open his arms to protect all of God's people and embrace with tender affection the whole of humanity, especially the poorest, the weakest, the least important, those whom Matthew lists in the final judgment on love: the hungry, the thirsty, the stranger, the naked, the sick, and those in prison (cf. Matt 25:31–46). Only those who serve with love are able to protect!

In the second reading, Saint Paul speaks of Abraham, who, "hoping against hope, believed" (Rom 4:18). Hoping against hope! Today, too, amid so much darkness, we need to see the light of hope and to be men and women who bring hope to others. To protect creation, to protect every man and every woman, to look upon them with tenderness and love, is to open up a horizon of hope; it is to let a shaft of light break through the heavy clouds; it is to bring the warmth of hope! For believers, for us Christians, like Abraham, like Saint Joseph, the hope that we bring is set against the horizon of God, which has opened up before us in Christ. It is a hope built on the rock, which is God.

To protect Jesus with Mary, to protect the whole of creation, to protect each person, especially the poorest, to protect ourselves: this is a service that the Bishop of Rome is called to carry out, yet, one to which all of us are called, so that the star of hope will shine brightly. Let us protect with love all that God has given us!

I implore the intercession of the Virgin Mary, Saint Joseph, Saints Peter and Paul, and Saint Francis, that the Holy Spirit may accompany my ministry, and I ask all of you to pray for me! Amen.

VIII

Audience with Representatives of the Churches and Ecclesial Communities and of the Different Religions

Dear Brothers and Sisters,

Before all else, I express my heartfelt thanks for what my brother Andrew [Ecumenical Patriarch Bartholomaios I] has said to us. Many thanks! Many thanks!

It is a source of particular joy for me to meet today with you, the delegates of the Orthodox Churches, of the Oriental Orthodox Churches, and of the Ecclesial Communities of the West. I thank you for taking part in the celebration which marked the beginning of my ministry as the Bishop of Rome and the Successor of Peter.

Yesterday morning, during Holy Mass, through you, I felt the spiritual presence of the communities which you represent. In this expression of faith, it seemed that we were experiencing all the more urgently the prayer for unity between believers in Christ and, at the same time, seeing prefigured in some way its full realization, which depends on God's plan and our own faithful cooperation.

I begin my apostolic ministry during this year which my venerable predecessor Benedict XVI, with truly inspired intuition, proclaimed for the Catholic Church as a Year of Faith. With this initiative, which I wish to continue and which I trust will prove a stimulus for our common journey of faith, he wanted to mark the fiftieth anniversary of the beginning of the Second Vatican Council by proposing a sort of pilgrimage toward what all Christians consider essential: the personal, transforming encounter with Jesus Christ, the Son of God, who died and rose for our salvation. The core message of the Council is found precisely in the desire to proclaim this perennially valid treasure of faith to the men and women of our time.

Along with you, I cannot forget all that the Council meant for the progress of ecumenism. Here I would like to recall the words of Blessed John XXIII, the fiftieth anniversary of whose death we shall soon celebrate, in his memorable opening address: "The Catholic Church considers it her duty to work actively for the fulfillment of the great mystery of that unity for which Jesus Christ prayed so earnestly to his heavenly Father on the eve of his great sacrifice; the knowledge that she is so intimately associated with that prayer is for her an occasion of ineffable peace and joy" (AAS 54 [1962], 793). These were the words of Pope John.

Yes, dear brothers and sisters in Christ, let us all feel closely united to the prayer of our Savior at the Last Supper, to his appeal: *ut unum sint*. Let us ask the Father of mercies to enable us to live fully the faith graciously bestowed upon us on the day of our Baptism and to bear witness to it freely, joyfully, and courageously. This will be the best service we can offer to the cause of Christian unity, a service of hope for a world still torn by divisions, conflicts, and rivalries. The more we are faithful to his will, in our thoughts, words, and actions, the more we will progress, really and substantially, toward unity.

For my part, I wish to assure you that, in continuity with

my predecessors, it is my firm intention to pursue the path of ecumenical dialogue, and I thank the Pontifical Council for Promoting Christian Unity for the help that it continues to provide, in my name, in the service of this most noble cause. I ask you, dear brothers and sisters, to bring my cordial greetings and the assurance of my prayerful remembrance in the Lord Jesus to the Christian communities which you represent, and I beg of you the charity of a special prayer for me, that I may be a pastor according to the heart of Christ.

And now I turn to you, the distinguished representatives of the Jewish people, to whom we are linked by a most special spiritual bond, since, as the Second Vatican Council stated, "the Church of Christ recognizes that in God's plan of salvation the beginnings of her faith and her election are to be found in the patriarchs, Moses and the prophets" (*Nostra Aetate*, 4). I thank you for your presence and I trust that, with the help of the Most High, we can make greater progress in that fraternal dialogue which the Council wished to encourage (cf. ibid.) and which has indeed taken place, bearing no little fruit, especially in recent decades.

I also greet and cordially thank all of you, dear friends, who are followers of other religious traditions; first Muslims, who worship God as one, living and merciful, and invoke him in prayer, and all of you. I greatly appreciate your presence: in it, I see a tangible sign of a will to grow in mutual esteem and in cooperation for the common good of humanity.

The Catholic Church is conscious of the importance of promoting friendship and respect between men and women of different religious traditions—I want to repeat this: promoting friendship and respect between men and women of different religious traditions—a sign of this can be seen in the important work carried out by the Pontifical Council for Interreligious Dialogue. The Church is likewise conscious of the responsibility which all of us have for our world, for the whole of creation, which we must love and protect. There is much that we can do to benefit the poor, the needy, and those who suffer, and to favor justice, promote reconciliation, and build peace. But before all else, we need to keep alive in our world the thirst for the absolute, and to counter the dominance of a one-dimensional vision of the human person, a vision which reduces human beings to what they produce and to what they consume: this is one of the most insidious temptations of our time.

We know how much violence has resulted in recent times from the attempt to eliminate God and the divine from the horizon of humanity, and we are aware of the importance of witnessing in our societies to that primordial openness to transcendence which lies deep within the human heart. In this, we also sense our closeness to all those men and women who, although not identifying themselves as followers of any religious tradition, are nonetheless searching for truth, goodness, and beauty—the truth, goodness, and beauty of God. They are our valued allies in the commitment to defending human dignity, in building a peaceful coexistence between peoples, and in safeguarding and caring for creation.

Dear friends, once again, I thank you for your presence. I offer all of you my heartfelt, fraternal good wishes.

IX

Audience with the Diplomatic Corps Accredited to the Holy See

Your Excellencies,
Ladies and Gentlemen,

Heartfelt thanks to your Dean, Ambassador Jean-Claude Michel, for the kind words that he has addressed to me in the name of everyone present. It gives me joy to welcome you for this exchange of greetings: a simple, yet, deeply felt ceremony that somehow seeks to express the Pope's embrace of the world. Through you, indeed, I encounter your peoples, and thus in a sense, I can reach out to every one of your fellow citizens, with their joys, their troubles, their expectations, their desires.

Your presence here in such numbers is a sign that the relations between your countries and the Holy See are fruitful, that they are truly a source of benefit to mankind. That, indeed, is what matters to the Holy See: the good of every person upon this earth! And it is with this understanding that the Bishop of Rome embarks upon his ministry, in the knowledge that he can count on the friendship and affection of the countries you represent, and in the certainty that you share this objective. At the same time, I hope that it will also be an opportunity to begin a journey with those few countries that do not yet have diplomatic relations with the Holy

See, some of which were present at the Mass for the beginning of my ministry, or sent messages as a sign of their closeness—for which I am truly grateful.

As you know, there are various reasons why I chose the name of Francis of Assisi, a familiar figure far beyond the borders of Italy and Europe, even among those who do not profess the Catholic faith. One of the first reasons was Francis' love for the poor. How many poor people there still are in the world! And what great suffering they have to endure! After the example of Francis of Assisi, the Church in every corner of the globe has always tried to care for and look after those who suffer from want, and I think that, in many of your countries, you can attest to the generous activity of Christians who dedicate themselves to helping the sick, orphans, the homeless and all the marginalized, thus, striving to make society more humane and more just.

But there is another form of poverty! It is the spiritual poverty of our time, which afflicts the so-called richer countries particularly seriously. It is what my much-loved predecessor, Benedict XVI, called the "tyranny of relativism," which makes everyone his own criterion and endangers the coexistence of peoples. And that brings me to a second reason for my name. Francis of Assisi tells us we should work to build peace. But there is no true peace without truth! There cannot be true peace if everyone is his own criterion, if everyone can always claim exclusively his own rights, without at the same time caring for the good of others, of everyone, on the basis of the nature that unites every human being on this earth.

One of the titles of the Bishop of Rome is Pontiff, that is, a builder of bridges with God and between people. My wish is that the dialogue between us should help to build bridges connecting all people, in such a way that everyone can see in the other, not an enemy, not a rival, but a brother or sister to be welcomed and embraced! My own origins impel me to work for the building of bridges. As you know, my family is of Italian origin; and so this dialogue between places and cultures a great distance apart matters greatly to me, this dialogue between one end of the world and the other, which today are growing ever closer, more interdependent, more in need of opportunities to meet and to create real spaces of authentic fraternity.

In this work, the role of religion is fundamental. It is not possible to build bridges between people while forgetting God. But the converse is also true: it is not possible to establish true links with God, while ignoring other people. Hence, it is important to intensify dialogue among the various religions, and I am thinking particularly of dialogue with Islam. At the Mass marking the beginning of my ministry, I greatly appreciated the presence of so many civil and religious leaders from the Islamic world. And it is also important to intensify outreach to nonbelievers, so that the differences which divide and hurt us may never prevail, but rather the desire to build true links of friendship between all peoples, despite their diversity.

Fighting poverty, both material and spiritual, building peace, and constructing bridges: these, as it were, are the reference points for a journey that I want to invite each of the countries here represented to take up. But it is a difficult journey, if we do not learn to grow in love for this world of ours. Here, too, it helps me to think of the name of Francis, who teaches us profound respect for the whole of creation and the protection of our environment, which all too often, instead of using for the good, we exploit greedily, to one another's detriment.

Dear Ambassadors,
Ladies and Gentlemen,

Thank you again for all the work that you do, alongside the Secretariat of State, to build peace and construct bridges of friendship and fraternity. Through you, I would like to renew to your Governments my thanks for their participation in the celebrations on the occasion of my election, and my heartfelt desire for a fruitful common endeavor. May Almighty God pour out his gifts on each one of you, on your families and on the peoples that you represent.

Thank you!

X

Celebration of Palm Sunday of the Passion of Our Lord

Jesus enters Jerusalem. The crowd of disciples accompanies him in festive mood, their garments are stretched out before him, there is talk of the miracles he has accomplished, and loud praises are heard: "Blessed is the King who comes in the name of the Lord. Peace in heaven and glory in the highest!" (Luke 19:38).

Crowds, celebrating, praise, blessing, peace: joy fills the air. Jesus has awakened great hopes, especially in the hearts of the simple, the humble, the poor, the forgotten, those who do not matter in the eyes of the world. He understands human sufferings, he has shown the face of God's mercy, and he has bent down to heal body and soul.

This is Jesus. This is his heart, which looks to all of us, to our sicknesses, to our sins. The love of Jesus is great. And, thus, he enters Jerusalem, with this love, and looks at us. It is a beautiful scene, full of light—the light of the love of Jesus, the love of his heart—of joy, of celebration.

At the beginning of Mass, we too repeated it. We waved our palms, our olive branches. We too welcomed Jesus; we too expressed our joy at accompanying him, at knowing him to be close, present in us and among us as a friend, a brother, and also as a King: that is, a shining beacon for our lives. Jesus is God, but he lowered himself to walk with us.

He is our friend, our brother. He illumines our path here. And in this way, we have welcomed him today. And here the first word that I wish to say to you: joy! Do not be men and women of sadness: a Christian can never be sad! Never give way to discouragement! Ours is not a joy born of having many possessions, but from having encountered a Person: Jesus, in our midst; it is born from knowing that with him we are never alone, even at difficult moments, even when our life's journey comes up against problems and obstacles that seem insurmountable, and there are so many of them! And in this moment, the enemy, the devil, comes, often disguised as an angel, and slyly speaks his word to us. Do not listen to him! Let us follow Jesus! We accompany, we follow Jesus, but above all, we know that he accompanies us and carries us on his shoulders. This is our joy, this is the hope that we must bring to this world. Please do not let yourselves be robbed of hope! Do not let hope be stolen! The hope that Jesus gives us.

The second word. Why does Jesus enter Jerusalem? Or better: how does Jesus enter Jerusalem? The crowds acclaim him as King. And he does not deny it, he does not tell them to be silent (cf. Luke 19:39–40). But what kind of a King is Jesus? Let us take a look at him: he is riding on a donkey, he is not accompanied by a court, he is not surrounded by an army as a symbol of power. He is received by humble people, simple folk who have the sense to see something more in Jesus; they have that sense of the faith, which says: here is the Savior. Jesus does not enter the Holy City to receive the honors reserved to earthly kings, to the powerful, to rulers; he enters to be scourged, insulted, and abused, as Isaiah foretold in the First Reading (cf. Isa 50:6). He enters to receive a crown of thorns, a staff, a purple robe: his kingship becomes an object of derision. He enters to climb Calvary, carrying his burden of wood. And this brings us to the second word: Cross. Jesus enters Jerusalem in order to die on the Cross. And it is precisely here that his kingship shines forth in godly fashion: his royal throne is the wood of the Cross! It reminds me of what Benedict XVI said to the Cardinals: you are princes, but of a king crucified. That is the throne of Jesus. Jesus takes it upon himself…Why the Cross? Because Jesus takes upon himself the evil, the filth, the sin of the world, including the sin of all of us, and he cleanses it, he cleanses it with his blood, with the mercy and the love of God. Let us look around: how many wounds are inflicted upon humanity by evil! Wars, violence, economic conflicts that hit the weakest, greed for money that you can't take with you and have to leave. When we were small, our grandmother used to say: a shroud has no pocket. Love of power, corruption, divisions, crimes against human life and against creation! And—as each one of us knows and is aware—our personal sins: our failures in love and respect toward God, toward our neighbor, and toward the whole of creation. Jesus on the Cross feels the whole weight of the evil, and with the force of God's, love he conquers it, he defeats it with his resurrection. This is the good that Jesus does for us on the throne of the Cross. Christ's Cross embraced with love never leads to sadness, but to joy, to the joy of having been saved and of doing a little of what he did on the day of his death.

Today, in this Square, there are many young people: for twenty-eight years, Palm Sunday has been World Youth Day! This is our third word: youth! Dear young people, I saw you in the procession as you were coming in; I think of you celebrating around Jesus, waving your olive branches. I think of you crying out his name and expressing your joy at being with him! You have an important part in the celebration of faith! You bring us the joy of faith and you tell us that we must live the faith with a young heart, always: a young heart, even at the age of seventy or eighty. Dear young people! With Christ, the heart never grows old! Yet, all of us, all of you know very well that the King whom we follow and who accompanies us is very special: he is a King who loves even to the Cross and who teaches us to serve and to love. And you are not ashamed of his Cross! On the contrary, you embrace it, because you have understood that it is in giving ourselves, in emerging from ourselves that we have true joy and that, with his love, God conquered evil. You carry the pilgrim Cross through all the continents, along the highways of the world! You carry it in response to Jesus' call: "Go, make disciples of all nations" (Matt 28:19), which is the theme of World Youth Day this year. You carry it so as to tell everyone that, on the Cross, Jesus knocked down the wall of enmity that divides people and nations, and he brought reconciliation and peace. Dear friends, I too am setting out on a journey with you, starting today, in the footsteps of Blessed John Paul II and Benedict XVI. We are already close to the next stage of this great pilgrimage of the Cross. I look forward joyfully to next July in Rio de Janeiro! I will see you in that great city in Brazil! Prepare well—prepare spiritually above all—in your communities, so that our gathering in Rio may be a sign of faith for the whole world. Young people must say to the world: to follow Christ is good; to go with Christ is good; the message of Christ is good; emerging from ourselves, to the ends of the earth and of existence, to take Jesus there, is good! Three points, then: joy, Cross, young people.

Let us ask the intercession of the Virgin Mary. She teaches us the joy of meeting Christ, the love with which we must look to the foot of the Cross, the enthusiasm of the young heart with which we must follow him during this Holy Week and throughout our lives. May it be so.

XI

Angelus

Dear Brothers and Sisters,

At the end of this celebration, we invoke the intercession of the Virgin Mary, that she may accompany us during Holy Week. May she, who followed her Son with faith all the way to Calvary, help us to walk behind him, carrying his Cross with serenity and love, so as to attain the joy of Easter. May Our Lady of Sorrows support especially those who are experiencing difficult situations. My thoughts turn to the people afflicted with tuberculosis, as today is the World Day against this disease. To Mary, I entrust especially you, dear young people, and your path toward Rio de Janeiro.

Until July in Rio [for World Youth Day]! Prepare your hearts spiritually.

I wish you all much joy on your journey!

V. The Angel of the Lord declared unto Mary.
R. And she conceived of the Holy Spirit.

Hail, Mary, full of grace, the Lord is with thee.
Blessed art thou among women,
and blessed is the fruit of thy womb, Jesus.
Holy Mary, Mother of God,

pray for us sinners,
now and at the hour of our death. Amen.

V. Behold the handmaid of the Lord.
R. Be it done unto me according to thy word.

Hail Mary.

V. And the Word was made flesh.
R. And dwelt among us.

Hail Mary.

V. Pray for us, O holy Mother of God.
R. That we may be made worthy of the promises of Christ.

Let us pray;
Pour forth, we beseech thee, O Lord, thy grace into our hearts; that we, to whom the Incarnation of Christ, thy Son, was made known by the message of an angel, may by his Passion and Cross be brought to the glory of his Resurrection. Through the same Christ, our Lord.
Amen.

Glory be to the Father
and to the Son
and to the Holy Spirit,
as it was in the beginning
is now, and ever shall be
world without end. Amen.

XII

General Audience

Brothers and Sisters, Good Morning!

I am glad to welcome you to my first General Audience. With deep gratitude and reverence, I take up the "witness" from the hands of Benedict XVI, my beloved predecessor. After Easter, we shall resume the Catecheses for the Year of Faith. Today, I would like to reflect a little on Holy Week. We began this Week with Palm Sunday—the heart of the whole Liturgical Year—in which we accompany Jesus in his Passion, death, and Resurrection.

But what does living Holy Week mean to us? What does following Jesus on his journey to Calvary on his way to the Cross and the Resurrection mean? In his earthly mission, Jesus walked the roads of the Holy Land; he called twelve simple people to stay with him, to share his journey, and to continue his mission. He chose them from among the people full of faith in God's promises. He spoke to all without distinction: the great and the lowly, the rich young man and the poor widow, the powerful, and the weak; he brought God's mercy and forgiveness; he healed, he comforted, he understood; he gave hope; he brought to all the presence of God who cares for every man and every woman, just as a good father and a good mother care for each one of their children.

God does not wait for us to go to him but it is he who moves toward us, without calculation, without quantification. That is what God is like. He always takes the first step, he comes toward us.

Jesus lived the daily reality of the most ordinary people: he was moved as he faced the crowd that seemed like a flock without a shepherd; he wept before the sorrow that Martha and Mary felt at the death of their brother, Lazarus; he called a publican to be his disciple; he also suffered betrayal by a friend. In him, God has given us the certitude that he is with us, he is among us. "Foxes," he, Jesus, said, "have holes, and birds of the air have nests, but the Son of man has nowhere to lay his head" (Matt 8:20). Jesus has no house, because his house is the people, it is we who are his dwelling place, his mission is to open God's doors to all, to be the presence of God's love.

In Holy Week, we live the crowning moment of this journey, of this plan of love that runs through the entire history of the relations between God and humanity. Jesus enters Jerusalem to take his last step with which he sums up the whole of his existence. He gives himself without reserve, he keeps nothing for himself, not even life. At the Last Supper, with his friends, he breaks the bread and passes the cup round "for us." The Son of God offers himself to us, he puts his Body and his Blood into our hands, so as to be with us always, to dwell among us. And in the Garden of Olives, and likewise in the trial before Pilate, he puts up no resistance, he gives himself; he is the suffering Servant, foretold by Isaiah, who empties himself, even unto death (cf. Isa 53:12).

Jesus does not experience this love that leads to his sacrifice passively or as a fatal destiny. He does not, of course, conceal his deep human distress as he faces a violent death, but with absolute trust, commends himself to the Father. Jesus gave himself up to death voluntarily in order to reciprocate the love of God the Father, in perfect union with his will, to demonstrate his love for us. On the Cross, Jesus "loved me and gave himself for me" (Gal 2:20). Each one of us can say: "he loved me and gave himself for me." Each one can say this, "for me."

What is the meaning of all this for us? It means that this is my, your, and our road, too. Living Holy Week, following Jesus not only with the emotion of the heart; living Holy Week, following Jesus means learning to come out of ourselves—as I said last Sunday—in order to go to meet others, to go toward the outskirts of existence, to be the first to take a step toward our brothers and our sisters, especially those who are the most distant, those who are forgotten, those who are most in need of understanding, comfort, and help. There is such a great need to bring the living presence of Jesus, merciful and full of love!

Living Holy Week means entering ever more deeply into the logic of God, into the logic of the Cross, which is not primarily that of suffering and death, but rather that of love and of the gift of self which brings life. It means entering into the logic of the Gospel. Following and accompanying Christ, staying with him, demands "coming out of ourselves," requires us to be outgoing; to come out of ourselves, out of a dreary way of living faith that has become a habit, out of the temptation to withdraw into our own plans, which end by shutting out God's creative action.

God came out of himself to come among us, he pitched his tent among us to bring to us his mercy that saves and gives hope. Nor must we be satisfied with staying in the pen of the ninety-nine sheep if we want to follow him and to remain with him; we too must "go out" with him to seek the lost sheep, the one that has strayed the furthest. Be sure to remember: coming out of ourselves, just as Jesus, just as God came out of himself in Jesus and Jesus came out of himself for all of us.

Someone might say to me: "but Father, I don't have time," "I have so many things to do," "it's difficult," "what can I do with my feebleness and my sins, with so many things?" We are often satisfied with a few prayers, with a distracted and sporadic participation in Sunday Mass, with a few charitable acts; but we do not have the courage "to come out" to bring Christ to others. We are a bit like St. Peter. As soon as Jesus speaks of his Passion, death, and Resurrection, of the gift of himself, of love for all, the Apostle takes him aside and reproaches him. What Jesus says upsets his plans, seems unacceptable, threatens the security he had built for himself, his idea of the Messiah. And Jesus looks at his disciples and addresses to Peter what may possibly be the harshest words in the Gospels: "Get behind me Satan! For you are not on the side of God, but of men" (Mark 8:33). God always thinks with mercy: do not forget this. God always thinks mercifully. He is the merciful Father! God thinks like the father waiting for the son and goes to meet him, he spots him coming when he is still far off....

What does this mean? That he went every day to see if his son was coming home: this is our merciful Father. It indicates that he was waiting for him with longing on the terrace of his house. God thinks like the Samaritan who did not pass by the unfortunate man, pitying him or looking at him from the other side of the road, but helped him without asking for anything in return; without asking whether he was a Jew, a pagan, or a Samaritan, whether he was rich or poor: he asked for nothing. He went to help him: God is like this. God thinks like the shepherd who lays down his life in order to defend and save his sheep.

Holy Week is a time of grace, which the Lord gives us to open the doors of our heart, of our life, of our parishes—what a pity so many parishes are closed!—of the movements, of the associations; and "to come out" in order to meet others, to make ourselves close, to bring them the light and joy of our faith. To come out always! And to do so with God's love and tenderness, with respect and with patience, knowing that God takes our hands, our feet, our heart, and guides them and makes all our actions fruitful.

I hope that we all will live these days well, following the Lord courageously; carrying within us a ray of his love for all those we meet.

GREETINGS

Heartfelt greetings to the English-speaking pilgrims, especially the large group of university students taking part in the international UNIV Congress here in Rome. I extend a warm welcome to the pilgrims from England, Ireland, the Philippines, and the United States of America. I invite all of you to enter fully into the spirit of Holy Week, following in the footsteps of Jesus and bringing the light of his love to everyone you meet. Happy Easter!

APPEAL

I am closely following what is happening at this time in the Central African Republic, and I wish to assure you of my prayers for all those who suffer, especially for the relatives of the victims, the injured, and the people who have lost their homes and were forced to flee. I call for an immediate halt to the violence and looting and to find a political solution as quickly as possible to the crisis, restoring peace and harmony in that beloved country, for too long marked by conflict and division.

XIII

Chrism Mass

READINGS

FIRST READING

Isaiah 61:1–3a, 6a, 8b–9

The spirit of the LORD has been given to me, for the LORD has anointed me. He has sent me to bring good news to the poor, to bind up hearts that are broken; to proclaim liberty to captives, freedom to those in prison; to proclaim a year of favor from the LORD, a day of vengeance for our God; to comfort all those who mourn and to give them for ashes a garland; for mourning robe the oil of gladness, for despondency, praise. But you, you will be named "priests of the LORD", they will call you "ministers of our God". I reward them faithfully and make an everlasting covenant with them. Their race will be famous throughout the nations, their descendants throughout the peoples. All who see them will admit that they are a race whom the LORD has blessed.

PSALM

Psalm 88

I have found David my servant and with my holy oil anointed him. My hand shall always be with him and my arm shall make him strong.

My truth and my love shall be with him; by my name his might shall be exalted. He will say to me: "You are my father, my God, the rock who saves me."

SECOND READING

Revelation 5:1–8

Grace and peace to you from Jesus Christ, the faithful witness, the First-born from the dead, the Ruler of the kings of the earth. He loves us and has washed away our sins with his blood, and made us a line of kings, priests to serve his God and Father; to him, then, be glory and power for ever and ever. Amen. It is he who is coming on the clouds; everyone will see him, even those who pierced him, and all the races of the earth will mourn over him. This is the truth. Amen. "I am the Alpha and the Omega" says the Lord God, who is, who was, and who is to come, the Almighty.

GOSPEL

Luke 4:16–21

Jesus came to Nazareth, where he had been brought up, and went into the synagogue on the Sabbath day as he usually did. He stood up to read, and they handed him the scroll of the prophet Isaiah. Unrolling the scroll he found the place where it is written:

The spirit of the Lord has been given to me, for he has anointed me. He has sent me to bring the good news to the poor, to proclaim liberty to captives and to the blind new sight, to set the downtrodden free, to proclaim the Lord's year of favor.

He then rolled up the scroll, gave it back to the assistant and sat down. And all eyes in the synagogue were fixed on him. Then he began to speak to them, "This text is being fulfilled today even as you listen."

HOMILY

Dear Brothers and Sisters,

This morning, I have the joy of celebrating my first Chrism Mass as the Bishop of Rome. I greet all of you with affection, especially you, dear priests, who, like myself, today recall the day of your ordination.

The readings and the Psalm of our Mass speak of God's "anointed ones": the suffering Servant of Isaiah, King David, and Jesus our Lord. All three have this in common: the anointing that they receive is meant, in turn, to anoint God's faithful people, whose servants they are; they are anointed for the poor, for prisoners, for the oppressed…A fine image of this "being for" others can be found in the Psalm 133: "It is like the precious oil upon the head, running down upon the beard, on the beard of Aaron, running down upon the collar of his robe" (v. 2). The image of spreading oil, flowing down from the beard of Aaron upon the collar of his sacred robe, is an image of the priestly anointing which, through Christ, the Anointed One, reaches the ends of the earth, represented by the robe.

The sacred robes of the High Priest are rich in symbolism. One such symbol is that the names of the children of Israel were engraved on the onyx stones mounted on the shoulder-pieces of the ephod, the ancestor of our present-day chasuble: six on the stone of the right shoulder-piece and six on that of the left (cf. Exod 28:6–14). The names of the twelve tribes of Israel were also engraved on the breastplate (cf. Exod 28:21). This means that the priest celebrates by carrying on his shoulders the people entrusted to his care and bearing their names written in his heart. When we put on our simple chasuble, it might well make us feel, upon our shoulders and in our hearts, the burdens and the faces of our faithful people, our saints, and martyrs who are numerous in these times.

From the beauty of all these liturgical things, which is not so much about trappings and fine fabrics than about the glory of our God resplendent in his people, alive and strengthened, we turn now to a consideration of activity, action. The precious oil which anoints the head of Aaron does more than simply lend fragrance to his person; it overflows down to "the edges." The Lord will say this clearly: his anointing is meant for the poor, prisoners, and the sick, for those who are sorrowing and alone. My dear brothers, the ointment is not intended just to make us fragrant, much less to be kept in a jar, for then it would become rancid...and the heart bitter.

A good priest can be recognized by the way his people are anointed: this is a clear proof. When our people are anointed with the oil of gladness, it is obvious: for example, when they leave Mass looking as if they have heard good news. Our people like to hear the Gospel preached with "unction," they like it when the Gospel we preach touches their daily lives, when it runs down like the oil of Aaron to the edges of reality, when it brings light to moments of extreme darkness, to the "outskirts" where people of faith are most exposed to the onslaught of those who want to tear down their faith. People thank us because they feel that we have prayed over the realities of their everyday lives, their troubles, their joys, their burdens, and their hopes. And when they feel that the fragrance of the Anointed One, of Christ, has come to them through us, they feel encouraged to entrust to us everything they want to bring before the Lord: "Pray for me, Father, because I have this problem," "Bless me Father," "Pray for me"—these words are the sign that the anointing has flowed down to the edges of the robe, for it has turned into a prayer of supplication, the supplication of the People of God. When we have this relationship with God and with his people, and grace passes through us, then we are priests, mediators between God and men. What I want to emphasize is that we need constantly to stir up God's grace and perceive in every request, even those requests that are inconvenient and at times purely material or downright banal—but only apparently so—the desire of our people to be anointed with fragrant oil, since they know that we have it. To perceive and to sense, even as the Lord sensed the hope-filled anguish of the woman suffering from hemorrhages when she touched the hem of his garment. At that moment, Jesus, surrounded by people on every side, embodies all the beauty of Aaron vested in priestly raiment, with the oil running down upon his robes. It is a hidden beauty, one which shines forth only for those faith-filled eyes of the woman troubled with an issue of blood. But not even the disciples—future priests—see or understand: on the "existential outskirts," they see only what is on the surface: the crowd pressing in on Jesus from all sides (cf. Luke 8:42). The Lord, on the other hand, feels the power of the divine anointing which runs down to the edge of his cloak.

We need to "go out," then, in order to experience our own anointing, its power, and its redemptive efficacy: to the "outskirts" where there is suffering, bloodshed, blindness that longs for sight, and prisoners in thrall to many evil masters. It is not in soul-searching or constant introspection that we encounter the Lord: self-help courses can be useful in life, but to live our priestly life, going from one course to another, from one method to another, leads us to become Pelagians and to minimize the power of grace, which comes alive and flourishes to the extent that we, in faith, go out and give ourselves and the Gospel to others, giving what little ointment we have to those who have nothing, nothing at all.

The priest who seldom goes out of himself, who anoints little—I won't say "not at all" because, thank God, the people take the oil from us anyway—misses out on the best of our people, on what can stir the depths of his priestly heart. Those who do not go out of themselves, instead of being mediators, gradually become intermediaries, managers. We know the difference: the intermediary, the manager, "has already received his reward," and since he doesn't put his own skin and his own heart on the line, he never hears a warm, heartfelt word of thanks. This is precisely the reason for the dissatisfaction of some, who end up sad—sad priests—in some sense becoming collectors of antiques or novelties, instead of being shepherds living with "the odor of the sheep." This I ask you: Be shepherds, with the "odor of the sheep," make it real, as shepherds among your flock, fishers of men. True enough, the so-called crisis of priestly identity threatens us all and adds to the broader cultural crisis; but if we can resist its onslaught, we will be able to put out in the name of the Lord and cast our nets. It is not a bad thing that reality itself forces us to "put out into the deep," where what we are by grace is clearly seen as pure grace, out into the deep of the contemporary world, where the only thing that counts is "unction"—not function—and the nets which overflow with fish are those cast solely in the name of the One in whom we have put our trust: Jesus.

Dear lay faithful, be close to your priests with affection and with your prayers, that they may always be shepherds according to God's heart.

Dear priests, may God the Father renew in us the Spirit of holiness with whom we have been anointed. May he renew his Spirit in our hearts that this anointing may spread to everyone, even to those "outskirts" where our faithful people most look for it and most appreciate it. May our people sense that we are the Lord's disciples; may they feel that their names are written upon our priestly vestments and that we seek no other identity; and may they receive, through our words and deeds, the oil of gladness which Jesus, the Anointed One, came to bring us. Amen.

XIV

Homily for the Mass of the Lord's Supper

This is moving. Jesus, washing the feet of his disciples. Peter didn't understood it at all, he refused. But Jesus explained it for him. Jesus—God—did this! He, himself, explains to his disciples: "Do you know what I have done to you? You call me Teacher and Lord—and you are right, for that is what I am. So if I, your Lord and Teacher, have washed your feet, you also ought to wash one another's feet. For I have set you an example, that you also should do as I have done to you" (John 13:12–15).

It is the Lord's example: he is the most important, and he washes feet, because with us, what is highest must be at the service of others. This is a symbol, it is a sign, right? Washing feet means: "I am at your service." And with us, too, don't we have to wash each other's feet day after day? But what does this mean? That all of us must help one another. Sometimes I am angry with someone or other...but...let it go, let it go, and if he or she asks you a favor, do it.

Help one another: this is what Jesus teaches us and this is what I am doing, and doing with all my heart, because it is my duty. As a priest and a bishop, I must be at your service. But it is a duty which comes from my heart: I love it. I love this and I love to do it because that is what the Lord has taught me to do. But you, too, help one another:

help one another always. One another. In this way, by helping one another, we will do some good.

Now, we will perform this ceremony of washing feet, and let us think, let each one of us think: "Am I really willing, willing to serve, to help others?" Let us think about this, just this. And let us think that this sign is a caress of Jesus, which Jesus gives, because this is the real reason why Jesus came: to serve, to help us.

A QUESTION FROM A BOY

Thank you, Father, for coming today. But I want to ask one thing: Why did you come here today to Casal del Marmo?

THE HOLY FATHER'S RESPONSE

It is a feeling that came from the heart. Where are those who could help me to be more humble—to be a servant as I must be a bishop. And I have asked: "Where are those who would like a visit?" I thought, "Perhaps Casal del Marmo." When they told me, I came here.

But, really, it just came from the heart. Things the heart does do not have explanation [for], they just are.

Now I leave. Thank you very much for your welcome. Pray for me, and do not lose hope. Always look ahead!

Thank you very much!

XV

Way of the Cross at the Colosseum

Dear Brothers and Sisters,

Thank you for having taken part in these moments of deep prayer. I also thank those who have accompanied us through the media, especially the sick and elderly.

I do not wish to add too many words. One word should suffice this evening, that is, the Cross itself. The Cross is the word through which God has responded to evil in the world. Sometimes it may seem as though God does not react to evil, as if he is silent. And yet, God has spoken, he has replied, and his answer is the Cross of Christ: a word which is love, mercy, forgiveness. It also reveals a judgment, namely that God, in judging us, loves us. Let us remember this: God judges us by loving us. If I embrace his love, then I am saved, if I refuse it, then I am condemned, not by him, but my own self, because God never condemns, he only loves and saves.

Dear brothers and sisters, the word of the Cross is also the answer which Christians offer in the face of evil, the evil that continues to work in us and around us. Christians must respond to evil with good, taking the Cross upon themselves as Jesus did. This evening, we have heard the witness given by our Lebanese brothers and sisters: they composed these beautiful prayers and meditations. We extend our heartfelt gratitude to them for this work and for the witness they offer. We were able to see this when Pope Benedict visited Lebanon: we saw the beauty and the strong bond of communion joining Christians together in that land and the friendship of our Muslim brothers and sisters and so many others. That occasion was a sign to the Middle East and to the whole world: a sign of hope.

We now continue this Via Crucis in our daily lives. Let us walk together along the Way of the Cross and let us do so carrying in our hearts this word of love and forgiveness. Let us go forward, waiting for the Resurrection of Jesus, who loves us so much. He is all love!

XVI

Exposition of the Holy Shroud

Dear Brothers and Sisters,

I join all of you gathered before the Holy Shroud, and I thank the Lord who, through modern technology, offers us this possibility.

Even if it takes place in this way, we do not merely "look," but rather we venerate by a prayerful gaze. I would go further: we are, in fact, looked upon ourselves. This face has eyes that are closed, it is the face of one who is dead, and yet mysteriously he is watching us, and in silence he speaks to us. How is this possible? How is it that the faithful, like you, pause before this icon of a man scourged and crucified? It is because the Man of the Shroud invites us to contemplate Jesus of Nazareth. This image, impressed upon the cloth, speaks to our heart and moves us to climb the hill of Calvary, to look upon the wood of the Cross, and to immerse ourselves in the eloquent silence of love.

Let us, therefore, allow ourselves to be reached by this look, which is directed not to our eyes but to our heart. In silence, let us listen to what he has to say to us from beyond death itself. By means of the Holy Shroud, the unique and supreme Word of God comes to us: Love made man, incarnate in our history; the merciful love of God who has taken upon himself all the evil of the world to free us from its power. This disfigured face resembles all those faces of men and women marred by a life which does not respect their dignity, by war and violence which afflict the weakest...And yet, at the same time, the face in the Shroud conveys a great peace; this tortured body expresses a sovereign majesty. It is as if it let a restrained but powerful energy within it shine through, as if to say: have faith, do not lose hope; the power of the love of God, the power of the Risen One overcomes all things.

Looking upon the Man of the Shroud, I make my own the prayer which Saint Francis of Assisi prayed before the Crucifix:

Most High, glorious God,
enlighten the shadows of my heart,
and grant me a right faith, a certain hope and perfect charity,
sense and understanding, Lord,
so that I may accomplish your holy and true command. Amen.

XVII

Easter Vigil

Dear Brothers and Sisters,

In the Gospel of this radiant night of the Easter Vigil, we first meet the women who go to the tomb of Jesus with spices to anoint his body (cf. Luke 24:1–3). They go to perform an act of compassion, a traditional act of affection and love for a dear departed person, just as we would. They had followed Jesus, they had listened to his words, they had felt understood by him in their dignity, and they had accompanied him to the very end, to Calvary and to the moment when he was taken down from the cross. We can imagine their feelings as they make their way to the tomb: a certain sadness, sorrow that Jesus had left them, he had died, his life had come to an end. Life would now go on as before. Yet, the women continued to feel love, the love for Jesus, which now led them to his tomb. But at this point, something completely new and unexpected happens, something which upsets their hearts and their plans, something which will upset their whole life: they see the stone removed from before the tomb, they draw near, and they do not find the Lord's body. It is an event which leaves them perplexed, hesitant, full of questions: "What happened?" "What is the meaning of all this?" (cf. Luke 24:4). Doesn't the same thing also happen to us when something completely new occurs in our everyday life? We stop short, we don't understand, we don't know what to do. Newness often makes us fearful, including the newness which God brings us, the newness which God asks of us. We are like the Apostles in the Gospel: often we would prefer to hold on to our own security, to stand in front of a tomb, to think about someone who has died, someone who ultimately lives on only as a memory, like the great historical figures from the past. We are afraid of God's surprises. Dear brothers and sisters, we are afraid of God's surprises! He always surprises us! The Lord is like that.

Dear brothers and sisters, let us not be closed to the newness that God wants to bring into our lives! Are we often weary, disheartened, and sad? Do we feel weighed down by our sins? Do we think that we won't be able to cope? Let us not close our hearts, let us not lose confidence, let us never give up: there are no situations which God cannot change, there is no sin which he cannot forgive if only we open ourselves to him.

But let us return to the Gospel, to the women, and take one step further. They find the tomb empty, the body of Jesus is not there, something new has happened, but all this still doesn't tell them anything certain: it raises questions; it leaves them confused, without offering an answer. And suddenly there are two men in dazzling clothes who say: "Why do you look for the living among the dead? He is not here; but has risen" (Luke 24:5–6). What was a simple act, done surely out of love—going to the tomb—has now turned into an event, a truly life-changing event. Nothing remains as it was before, not only in the lives of those women, but also in our own lives and in the history of mankind. Jesus is not dead, he has risen, he is alive! He does not simply return to life; rather, he is life itself, because he is the Son of God, the living God (cf. Num 14:21–28; Deut 5:26; Josh 3:10). Jesus no longer belongs to the past, but lives in the present and is projected toward the future; Jesus is the everlasting "today" of God. This is how the newness of God appears to the women, the disciples, and all of us: as victory over sin, evil, and death, over everything that crushes life and makes it seem less human. And this is a message meant for me and for you dear sister, for you dear brother. How often does Love have to tell us: Why do you look for the living among the dead? Our daily problems and worries can wrap us up in ourselves, in sadness and bitterness...and that is where death is. That is not the place to look for the One who is alive! Let the risen Jesus enter your life, welcome him as a friend, with trust: he is life! If up till now you have kept him at a distance, step forward. He will receive you with open arms. If you have been indifferent, take a risk: you won't be disappointed. If following him seems difficult, don't be afraid, trust him, be confident that he is close to you, he is with you, and he will give you the peace you are looking for and the strength to live as he would have you do.

There is one last little element that I would like to emphasize in the Gospel for this Easter Vigil. The women encounter the newness of God. Jesus has risen, he is alive! But faced with the empty tomb and the two men in brilliant clothes, their first reaction is one of fear: "they were terrified and bowed their faces to the ground," Saint Luke tells us—they didn't even have courage to look. But when they hear the message of the Resurrection, they accept it in faith. And the two men in dazzling clothes tell them something of crucial importance: remember. "Remember what he told you when he was still in Galilee...And they remembered his words" (Luke 24:6, 8). This is the invitation to remember their encounter with Jesus, to remember his words, his actions, his life; and it is precisely this loving remembrance of their experience with the Master that enables the women to master their fear and to bring the message of the Resurrection to the Apostles and all the others (cf. Luke 24:9). To remember what God has done and continues to do for me, for us, to remember the road we have travelled; this is what opens our hearts to hope for the future. May we learn to remember everything that God has done in our lives.

On this radiant night, let us invoke the intercession of the Virgin Mary, who treasured all these events in her heart (cf. Luke 2:19, 51) and ask the Lord to give us a share in his Resurrection. May he open us to the newness that transforms, to the beautiful surprises of God. May he make us men and women capable of remembering all that he has done in our own lives and in the history of our world. May he help us to feel his presence as the one who is alive and at work in our midst. May he teach us each day, dear brothers and sisters, not to look among the dead for the Living One. Amen.

XVIII

Urbi et Orbi Message

Dear brothers and sisters in Rome and throughout the world,

Happy Easter! Happy Easter!

What a joy it is for me to announce this message: Christ is risen! I would like it to go out to every house and every family, especially where the suffering is greatest, in hospitals, in prisons…

Most of all, I would like it to enter every heart, for it is there that God wants to sow this Good News: Jesus is risen, there is hope for you, you are no longer in the power of sin, of evil! Love has triumphed, mercy has been victorious! The mercy of God always triumphs!

We, too, like the women who were Jesus' disciples, who went to the tomb and found it empty, may wonder what this event means (cf. Luke 24:4). What does it mean that Jesus is risen? It means that the love of God is stronger than evil and death itself; it means that the love of God can transform our lives and let those desert places in our hearts bloom. The love of God can do this!

This same love for which the Son of God became man and followed the way of humility and self-giving to the very end, down to hell—to the abyss of separation from God—this same merciful love has flooded with light the dead body of Jesus, has transfigured it, has made it pass into eternal life. Jesus did not return to his former life, to earthly life, but entered into the glorious life of God, and he entered there with our humanity, opening us to a future of hope.

This is what Easter is: it is the exodus, the passage of human beings from slavery to sin and evil to the freedom of love and goodness. Because God is life, life alone, and we are his glory: the living man (cf. Irenaeus, *Adversus Haereses*, 4, 20, 5–7).

Dear brothers and sisters, Christ died and rose once for all, and for everyone, but the power of the Resurrection, this Passover from slavery to evil to the freedom of goodness, must be accomplished in every age, in our concrete existence, in our everyday lives. How many deserts, even today, do human beings need to cross! Above all, the desert within, when we have no love for God or neighbor, when we fail to realize that we are guardians of all that the Creator has given us and continues to give us. God's mercy can make even the driest land become a garden, can restore life to dry bones (cf. Ezek 37:1–14).

So this is the invitation which I address to everyone: Let us accept the grace of Christ's Resurrection! Let us be renewed by God's mercy, let us be loved by Jesus, let us enable the power of his love to transform our lives, too; and let us become agents of this mercy, channels through which God can water the earth, protect all creation, and make justice and peace flourish.

And so we ask the risen Jesus, who turns death into life, to change hatred into love, vengeance into forgiveness, war into peace. Yes, Christ is our peace, and through him, we implore peace for all the world.

Peace for the Middle East, and particularly between Israelis and Palestinians, who struggle to find the road of agreement, that they may willingly and courageously resume negotiations to end a conflict that has lasted all too long.

Peace in Iraq, that every act of violence may end, and above all, for dear Syria, for its people torn by conflict and for the many refugees who await help and comfort. How much blood has been shed! And how much suffering must there still be before a political solution to the crisis will be found?

Peace for Africa, still the scene of violent conflicts. In Mali, may unity and stability be restored; in Nigeria, where attacks sadly continue, gravely threatening the lives of many innocent people, and where great numbers of persons, including children, are held hostage by terrorist groups. Peace in the East of the Democratic Republic of Congo, and in the Central African Republic, where many have been forced to leave their homes and continue to live in fear.

Peace in Asia, above all on the Korean peninsula: may disagreements be overcome and a renewed spirit of reconciliation grow.

Peace in the whole world, still divided by greed, looking for easy gain, wounded by the selfishness which threatens human life and the family, selfishness that continues in human trafficking, the most extensive form of slavery in this twenty-first century; human trafficking is the most extensive form of slavery in this twenty-first century! Peace to the whole world, torn apart by violence linked to drug trafficking and by the iniquitous exploitation of natural resources! Peace to this our Earth! May the risen Jesus bring comfort to the victims of natural disasters and make us responsible guardians of creation.

Dear brothers and sisters, to all of you who are listening to me, from Rome and from all over of the world, I address the invitation of the Psalm: "Give thanks to the LORD for he is good; for his steadfast love endures forever. Let Israel say: 'His steadfast love endures forever'" (Ps 118:1–2).

GREETING

Dear Brothers and Sisters, to you who have come from all over the world to this Square at the heart of Christianity, and to you linked by modern technology, I repeat my greeting: Happy Easter!

Bear in your families and in your countries the message of joy, hope, and peace, which every year, on this day, is powerfully renewed.

May the risen Lord, the conqueror of sin and death, be a support to you all, especially to the weakest and neediest. Thank you for your presence and for the witness of your faith. A thought and a special thank you for the beautiful flowers, which come from the Netherlands. To all of you, I affectionately say again: May the risen Christ guide all of you and the whole of humanity on the paths of justice, love, and peace.

XIX

Regina Caeli

Dear Brothers and Sisters,

Good Morning and a Happy Easter to you all! I thank you for coming here today, too, in such large numbers, to share in the joy of Easter, the central mystery of our faith. May the power of Christ's Resurrection reach every person—especially those who are suffering—and all the situations most in need of trust and hope.

Christ has fully triumphed over evil once and for all, but it is up to us, to the people of every epoch, to welcome this victory into our life and into the actual situations of history and society. For this reason, it seems to me important to emphasize what we ask God today in the liturgy. "O God, who give constant increase/to your Church by new offspring,/grant that your servants may hold fast in their lives/to the Sacrament they have received in faith" (Collect, Monday within the Octave of Easter).

It is true, yes, Baptism that makes us children of God and the Eucharist that unites us to Christ must become life, that is, they must be expressed in attitudes, behavior, gestures, and decisions. The grace contained in the Sacraments of Easter is an enormous potential for the renewal of our personal existence, of family life, of social relations. However, everything passes through the human heart: if I let myself be touched by the grace of the Risen Christ, if I let him change me in that aspect of mine which is not good, which can hurt me and others, I allow the victory of Christ to be affirmed in my life, to broaden its beneficial action. This is the power of grace! Without grace, we can do nothing. Without grace, we can do nothing! And with the grace of Baptism and of Eucharistic Communion, I can become an instrument of God's mercy, of that beautiful mercy of God.

To express in life the sacrament we have received: dear brothers and sisters, this is our daily duty, but I would also say our daily joy! The joy of feeling we are instruments of Christ's grace, like branches of the vine that is Christ himself, brought to life by the sap of his Spirit!

Let us pray together, in the name of the dead and Risen Lord and through the intercession of Mary Most Holy, that the Paschal Mystery may work profoundly within us and in our time so that hatred may give way to love, falsehood to truth, revenge to forgiveness, and sadness to joy.

AFTER THE REGINA CAELI

I greet you all with deep affection, dear pilgrims who have come from various continents to take part in this prayer meeting. I hope that each one of you may have a peaceful Easter Monday, the day on which the joyful proclamation of Easter rings out. Christ is Risen! Happy Easter to you all.

Happy Easter to you all and have a good lunch!

XX

General Audience

Dear Brothers and Sisters, Good Morning,

Today, let us take up the Catecheses of the Year of Faith. In the Creed, we repeat these words: "and rose again on the third day in accordance with the Scriptures." This is the very event that we are celebrating: the Resurrection of Jesus, the center of the Christian message, which has echoed from the beginning and was passed on so that it would come down to us. St Paul wrote to the Christians of Corinth: "I delivered to you as of first importance what I also received, that Christ died for our sins in accordance with the scriptures, that he was buried, that he was raised on the third day in accordance with the scriptures and that he appeared to Cephas, then to the Twelve" (1 Cor 15:3–5). This brief profession of faith proclaims the Paschal Mystery itself with the first appearances of the Risen One to Peter and the Twelve: the death and Resurrection of Jesus are the very heart of our hope.

Without this faith in the death and Resurrection of Jesus, our hope would be weak; but it would not even be hope; or precisely the death and Resurrection of Jesus are the heart of our hope. The Apostle said: "If Christ has not been raised, your faith is futile and you are still in your sins" (v. 17). Unfortunately, efforts have often been made to blur faith in the Resurrection of Jesus and doubts have crept in, even among believers. It is a little like that "rosewater" faith, as we say; it is not a strong faith. And this is due to superficiality and sometimes to indifference, busy as we are with a thousand things considered more important than faith, or because we have a view of life that is solely horizontal. However, it is the Resurrection itself that opens us to greater hope, for it opens our life and the life of the world to the eternal future of God, to full happiness, to the certainty that evil, sin, and death may be overcome. And this leads to living daily situations with greater trust, to facing them with courage and determination. Christ's Resurrection illuminates these everyday situations with a new light. The Resurrection of Christ is our strength!

But how was the truth of faith in Christ's Resurrection passed down to us? There are two kinds of testimony in the New Testament: some are in the form of a profession of faith, that is, of concise formulas that indicate the center of faith; while others are in the form of an account of the event of the Resurrection and of the facts connected with it.

The former, in the form of a profession of faith, for example, is the one we have just heard, or that of the Letter to the Romans in which St Paul wrote: "if you confess with your lips that 'Jesus is Lord!' and believe in your heart that God raised him from the dead, you will be saved" (10:9). From the Church's very first steps, faith in the Mystery of the death and Resurrection of Christ is firm and clear. Today, however, I would like to reflect on the latter, on the testimonies in the form of a narrative, which we find in the Gospels. First of all, let us note that the first witnesses of this event were the women. At dawn, they went to the tomb to anoint Jesus' body and found the first sign: the empty tomb (cf. Mark 16:1). Their meeting with a messenger of God followed. He announced: "Jesus of Nazareth, the Crucified One, has risen, he is not here" (cf. vv. 5–6). The women were motivated by love and were able to accept this announcement with faith: they believed and passed it on straight away, they did not keep it to themselves but passed it on.

They could not contain their joy in knowing that Jesus was alive, or the hope that filled their hearts. This should happen in our lives, too. Let us feel the joy of being Christian! We believe in the Risen One who conquered evil and death! Let us have the courage to "come out of ourselves" to take this joy and this light to all the places of our life! The Resurrection of Christ is our greatest certainty; he is our most precious treasure! How can we not share this treasure, this certainty with others? It is not only for us, it is to be passed on, to be shared with others. Our testimony is precisely this.

Another point: in the profession of faith in the New Testament, only men are recorded as witnesses of the Resurrection, the Apostles, but not the women. This is because, according to the Judaic Law of that time, women and children could not bear a trustworthy, credible witness. Instead, in the Gospels, women play a fundamental lead role. Here, we can grasp an element in favor of the historicity of the Resurrection: if it was an invented event, in the context of that time, it would not have been linked with the evidence of women. Instead, the Evangelists simply recounted what happened: women were the first witnesses. This implies that God does not choose in accordance with human criteria: the first witnesses of the birth of Jesus were shepherds, simple, humble people; the first witnesses of the Resurrection were women. And this is beautiful. This is part of the mission of women; of mothers, of women! Witnessing to their children, to their grandchildren, that Jesus is alive, is living, is risen. Mothers and women, carry on witnessing to this! It is the heart that counts for God, how open to him we are, whether we are like trusting children.

However, this also makes us think about how women, in the Church and on the journey of faith, had and still have today a special role in opening the doors to the Lord, in following him and in communicating his Face, for the gaze of faith is always in need of the simple and profound gaze of love.

The Apostles and disciples find it harder to believe. The women, not so. Peter runs to the tomb but stops at the empty tomb; Thomas has to touch the wounds on Jesus' body with his hands. On our way of faith, it is also important to know and to feel that God loves us and not to be afraid to love him. Faith is professed with the lips and with the heart, with words and with love.

After his appearances to the women, others follow. Jesus makes himself present in a new way, he is the Crucified One but his body is glorified; he did not return to earthly life but returned in a new condition. At first, they do not recognize him and it is only through his words and gestures that their eyes are opened. The meeting with the Risen One transforms, it gives faith fresh strength and a steadfast foundation. For us, too, there are many signs through which the Risen One makes himself known: Sacred Scripture, the Eucharist, the other Sacraments, charity, all those acts of love which bring a ray of the Risen One. Let us permit ourselves to be illuminated by Christ's Resurrection, let him transform us with his power, so that through us, too, the signs of death may give way to signs of life in the world.

I see that there are large numbers of young people in the square. There you are! I say to you: carry this certainty ahead: the Lord is alive and walks beside you through life. This is your mission! Carry this hope onward. May you be anchored to this hope: this anchor which is in heaven; hold the rope firmly, be anchored and carry hope forward. You, witnesses of Jesus, pass on the witness that Jesus is alive and this will give us hope, it will give hope to this world, which has aged somewhat, because of wars, because of evil, and because of sin. Press on, young people!

GREETINGS

I offer a warm welcome to all the English-speaking visitors present at today's Audience, including those from England, Scotland, Wales, Ireland, Norway, Sweden, Australia, the Philippines, Canada, and the United States. In a special way, I greet the newly ordained deacons from the Pontifical Irish College and their families. My greeting also goes to the delegation from the United States Senate. I thank the choirs for their praise of God in song. With great affection, I invoke upon all of you the joy and peace which are the abiding gifts of the Risen Lord.

I hope that you, dear young people, and you are many, may experience the living Jesus Christ, to become his witnesses. May you, dear sick people, feel the comfort of the Risen Lord's presence. And you, dear newlyweds, welcome him every day into your married life.

XXI
Biography

The first Pope of the Americas—Jorge Mario Bergoglio—hails from Argentina. The 76-year-old Jesuit Archbishop of Buenos Aires is a prominent figure throughout the continent, yet, remains a simple pastor who is deeply loved by his diocese, throughout which he has travelled extensively on the underground and by bus during the 15 years of his episcopal ministry.

"My people are poor and I am one of them," he has said more than once, explaining his decision to live in an apartment and cook his own supper. He has always advised his priests to show mercy and apostolic courage and to keep their doors open to everyone. The worst thing that could happen to the Church, he has said on various occasions, "is what de Lubac called spiritual worldliness," which means, "being self-centered." And when he speaks of social justice, he calls people first of all to pick up the Catechism, to rediscover the Ten Commandments and the Beatitudes. His project is simple: if you follow Christ, you understand that "trampling upon a person's dignity is a serious sin."

Despite his reserved character—his official biography consists of only a few lines, at least until his appointment as Archbishop of Buenos Aires—he became a reference point because of the strong stances he took during the dramatic financial crisis that overwhelmed the country in 2001.

He was born in Buenos Aires on 17 December 1936, the

son of Italian immigrants. His father, Mario, was an accountant employed by the railways and his mother, Regina Sivori, was a committed wife dedicated to raising their five children. He graduated as a chemical technician and then chose the path of the priesthood, entering the Diocesan Seminary of Villa Devoto. On 11 March 1958, he entered the novitiate of the Society of Jesus. He completed his studies of the humanities in Chile and returned to Argentina in 1963 to graduate with a degree in philosophy from the Colegio de San José in San Miguel. From 1964 to 1965, he taught literature and psychology at Immaculate Conception College in Santa Fé, and in 1966, he taught the same subject at the Colegio del Salvatore in Buenos Aires. From 1967–70, he studied theology and obtained a degree from the Colegio of San José.

On 13 December 1969, he was ordained a priest by Archbishop Ramón José Castellano. He continued his training between 1970 and 1971 at the University of Alcalá de Henares, Spain, and on 22 April 1973, made his final profession with the Jesuits. Back in Argentina, he was novice master at Villa Barilari, San Miguel; professor at the Faculty of Theology of San Miguel; consultor to the Province of the Society of Jesus and also Rector of the Colegio Máximo of the Faculty of Philosophy and Theology.

On 31 July 1973, he was appointed Provincial of the Jesuits in Argentina, an office he held for six years. He then resumed his work in the university sector and, from 1980 to 1986, served once again as Rector of the Colegio de San José, as well as parish priest, again in San Miguel. In March 1986, he went to Germany to finish his doctoral thesis; his superiors then sent him to the Colegio del Salvador in Buenos Aires and next to the Jesuit Church in the city of Córdoba as spiritual director and confessor.

It was Cardinal Antonio Quarracino, Archbishop of Buenos Aires, who wanted him as a close collaborator. So, on 20 May 1992, Pope John Paul II appointed him titular Bishop of Auca and Auxiliary of Buenos Aires. On 27 May, he received episcopal ordination from the Cardinal in the cathedral. He chose as his episcopal motto, *miserando atque eligendo*, and on his coat of, arms inserted the IHS, the symbol of the Society of Jesus.

He gave his first interview as a bishop to a parish newsletter, *Estrellita de Belém*. He was immediately appointed Episcopal Vicar of the Flores district and, on 21 December 1993, was also entrusted with the office of Vicar General of the Archdiocese. Thus, it came as no surprise when, on 3 June 1997, he was raised to the dignity of Coadjutor Archbishop of Buenos Aires. Not even nine months had passed when, upon the death of Cardinal Quarracino, he succeeded him on 28 February 1998, as Archbishop, Primate of Argentina and Ordinary for Eastern-rite faithful in Argentina who have no Ordinary of their own rite.

Three years later, at the Consistory of 21 February 2001, John Paul II created him Cardinal, assigning him the title of San Roberto Bellarmino. He asked the faithful not to come to Rome to celebrate his creation as Cardinal but rather to donate to the poor what they would have spent on the journey. As Grand Chancellor of the Catholic University of Argentina, he is the author of the books: *Meditaciones para religiosos* (1982), *Reflexiones sobre la vida apostólica* (1992), and *Reflexiones de esperanza* (1992).

In October 2001, he was appointed General Relator to the 10th Ordinary General Assembly of the Synod of Bishops on the Episcopal Ministry. This task was entrusted to him at the last minute to replace Cardinal Edward Michael Egan, Archbishop of New York, who was obliged to stay in his homeland because of the terrorist attacks on September 11th. At the Synod, he placed particular emphasis on "the prophetic mission of the bishop," his being a "prophet of justice," his duty to "preach ceaselessly" the social doctrine of the Church and also "to express an authentic judgment in matters of faith and morals."

All the while, Cardinal Bergoglio was becoming ever more popular in Latin America. Despite this, he never relaxed his sober approach or his strict lifestyle, which some have defined as almost "ascetic." In this spirit of poverty, he declined to be appointed as President of the Argentine Bishops' Conference in 2002, but three years later, he was elected and then, in 2008, reconfirmed for a further three-year mandate. Meanwhile, in April 2005, he took part in the Conclave in which Pope Benedict XVI was elected.

As Archbishop of Buenos Aires—a diocese with more than three million inhabitants—he conceived of a missionary project based on communion and evangelization. He had four main goals: open and brotherly communities, an informed laity playing a lead role, evangelization efforts addressed to every inhabitant of the city, and assistance to the poor and the sick. He aimed to re-evangelize Buenos Aires, "taking into account those who live there, its structure and its history." He asked priests and lay people to work together. In September 2009, he launched the solidarity campaign for the bicentenary of the Independence of the country. Two hundred charitable agencies are to be set up by 2016. And on a continental scale, he expected much from the impact of the message of the Aparecida Conference in 2007, to the point of describing it as the "*Evangelii Nuntiandi* of Latin America."

Until the beginning of the recent sede vacante, he was a member of the Congregation for Divine Worship and the Discipline of the Sacraments, the Congregation for the Clergy, the Congregation for Institutes of Consecrated Life and Societies of Apostolic Life, the Pontifical Council for the Family, and the Pontifical Commission for Latin America.

He was elected Supreme Pontiff on 13 March 2013.

Notes

I. APOSTOLIC BLESSING "URBI ET ORBI"; Central Loggia of St. Peter's Basilica; Wednesday, 13 March 2013.

II. "MISSA PRO ECCLESIA" WITH THE CARDINAL ELECTORS; HOMILY OF THE HOLY FATHER POPE FRANCIS; Sistine Chapel; Thursday, 14 March 2013.

III. AUDIENCE WITH THE COLLEGE OF CARDINALS; ADDRESS OF THE HOLY FATHER POPE FRANCIS; Clementine Hall; Friday, 15 March 2013.

IV. AUDIENCE TO REPRESENTATIVES OF THE COMMUNICATIONS MEDIA; ADDRESS OF THE HOLY FATHER POPE FRANCIS; Paul VI Audience Hall; Saturday, 16 March 2013.

V. HOLY MASS IN THE PARISH OF ST. ANNA IN THE VATICAN; HOMILY OF POPE FRANCIS; Fifth Sunday of Lent, 17 March 2013.

VI. ANGELUS; Saint Peter's Square; Sunday, 17 March 2013.

VII. MASS, IMPOSITION OF THE PALLIUM AND BESTOWAL OF THE FISHERMAN'S RING FOR THE BEGINNING OF THE PETRINE MINISTRY OF THE BISHOP OF ROME; HOMILY OF POPE FRANCIS; Saint Peter's Square; Tuesday, 19 March 2013; Solemnity of Saint Joseph.

VIII. AUDIENCE WITH REPRESENTATIVES OF THE CHURCHES AND ECCLESIAL COMMUNITIES AND OF THE DIFFERENT RELIGIONS; ADDRESS OF THE HOLY FATHER POPE FRANCIS; Clementine Hall; Wednesday, 20 March 2013.

IX. AUDIENCE WITH THE DIPLOMATIC CORPS ACCREDITED TO THE HOLY SEE; ADDRESS OF POPE FRANCIS; Sala Regia; Friday, 22 March 2013.

X. CELEBRATION OF PALM SUNDAY OF THE PASSION OF OUR LORD; HOMILY OF POPE FRANCIS; Saint Peter's Square; XXVIII World Youth Day; Sunday, 24 March 2013.

XI. ANGELUS; St Peter's Square; Palm Sunday, 24 March 2013.

XII. GENERAL AUDIENCE; Saint Peter's Square; Wednesday, 27 March 2013.

XIII. CHRISM MASS; HOMILY OF POPE FRANCIS; Saint Peter's Basilica; Holy Thursday, 28 March 2013.

XIV. MASS OF THE LORD'S SUPPER; HOMILY OF POPE FRANCIS; Prison for Minors "Casal del Marmo," Rome; Holy Thursday, 28 March 2013.

XV. WAY OF THE CROSS AT THE COLOSSEUM; ADDRESS OF POPE FRANCIS; Palatine Hill; Good Friday, 29 March 2013.

XVI. EXPOSITION OF THE HOLY SHROUD; VIDEO MESSAGE OF HIS HOLINESS POPE FRANCIS; Holy Saturday, 30 March 2013.

XVII. EASTER VIGIL; HOMILY OF POPE FRANCIS; Vatican Basilica; Holy Saturday, 30 March 2013.

XVIII. URBI ET ORBI MESSAGE OF POPE FRANCIS; EASTER 2013; Easter Sunday, 31 March 2013.

XIX. REGINA CÆLI; St. Peter's Square; Easter Monday, 1 April 2013.

XX. GENERAL AUDIENCE; Saint Peter's Square; Wednesday, 3 April 2013.